"As a psychotherapist working with families, I consider this book to be a significant contribution to healthy parent-child relationships. The deep appreciation for parents as well as children, as conveyed by Ms. Ross, is a fresh and compelling approach. The specific examples, presented with such clarity, and the author's use of her experiences with her own developing child, are personally moving, as well as highly instructive. This book is a gift to parents."

**— Shirley C. Lobley, M.A., L.P.C., L.M.F.T.,
Psychotherapist**

"As I think back upon the years when I was actively parenting, I perceive that my only successes were scored when (but inadvertently!) I hit upon one or more fragments of the techniques so cogently outlined in this book. It is a masterpiece. It proves that not only can "parenting wisdom" come in small packages, but so can a complete set of instructions for how to put it into practice."

**— Wallace L. Anderson, Sc.D.,
University of Houston**

"This book is chock full of interesting anecdotes which make it come alive to the reader, providing insight into the world of childhood. By lacing important skills with humor, Ms. Ross makes the acquisition of these principles and techniques easy to internalize and apply. This book is a must for parents and, indeed, for all those who work with young children."

**— Kim Yerly, M.Ed., L.P.C.,
Elementary School Counselor**

"*Practical Parenting* tackles the challenges that face every parent, from tantrums to averting the "bedtime blues." As a parent, I'm grateful for these easy-to-follow techniques that really work, taking some of the mystery and frustration out of the toughest job in the world."

**— Cheryl Wiles, Associate Director,
St. Bartholomew Community Club**

"Parenting . . . is often difficult. Julie Ross is a contributing option."

— The New York Big Apple Parents Paper

PRACTICAL
PARENTING

— FOR THE —

21ST CENTURY

THE MANUAL YOU WISH HAD
COME WITH YOUR CHILD

JULIE A. ROSS, M.A.

INTRODUCTION BY MICHAEL H. POPKIN, PH.D.

Excalibur Publishing
New York

Published by:
Excalibur Publishing
511 Avenue of the Americas, PMB 392
New York, New York 10011

Cover and graphic design: Kara Glasgold, Griffin Design
Author photo: Christine Butler

Library of Congress Cataloging in Publication Data

Ross, Julie A., date.
    Practical parenting for the 21st century : the manual you wish had
come with your child / Julie A. Ross ; introd. by Michael H. Popkin.
        p.   cm.
    Includes bibliographical references and index.
    ISBN 0-9627226-6-9 (paperback)
    1. Parenting--United States--Handbooks, manuals, etc. 2. Child
rearing--United States--Handbooks, manuals, etc.   I. Title.
HQ755.8.R675   1993   92-55103
649'.1'09730905--dc20   CIP

Printed in the United States of America

10 9 8 7

For my husband, Steve, my
life-partner and supportive co-parent,
and for Emilie, our daughter,
who gives us lots of practice
and an overabundance of joy.

TABLE OF CONTENTS

Acknowledgments

I'd like to thank my husband for his love and support, and for giving me the time I needed to think and write.

I'd like to thank my daughter for her patience, as I continue to grow as a parent.

Many thanks to my editor, whose advice, encouragement, and superb editing abilities greatly enhanced not only my book, but have enriched my life as well.

Thanks to all my "readers," whose contributions I greatly acknowledge. Their advice was invaluable to me, as I fine-tuned the manuscript.

Many thanks to my father, who has always encouraged me academically, and from whom I felt a great deal of support during the process of writing this book; and to my mother, who instilled within me a knowledge of my own self-worth and provided a role model worth living up to.

There are many others without whom this book would not have been possible — friends, family, professors, mentors, and of course, the parents in my workshops and support groups. The learning process is a two-way street, and I learn as much from them as they do from me.

I am grateful for the opportunity to continue to learn from those who come to me with questions. Their children are the future of this world, and because of their desire to be better, more conscientious parents, the future is very bright indeed.

Introduction

As I travel around the country talking about parent education, I often begin with a survey. I ask parents to raise their hands if they believe that parenting effectively is both important and difficult. Everyone raises their hands. I then ask them to raise their hands if they believe that parenting effectively is at least as important and difficult as being an effective waiter or waitress. They chuckle, then raise their hands. How about being an effective teacher, I ask. Again, the audience is quick to agree. Finally, I ask them if parenting effectively is as difficult and important as what I do, teaching parenting skills. And since I am also a parent myself, I am quick to assure them that it certainly is.

Then I ask the audience why it is that the only one of these four jobs for which we as a society provide no systematic training is the one that we all agree is the most important and difficult of all — that of preparing the next generation of children to run the planet. I know waiters and waitresses who get six-week training courses before they are ever allowed to bring food from the kitchen to a table — and then they do it with a more experienced server standing right behind them to offer support!

It seems to me that we have done a tremendous injustice to parents. We have treated the job of parenting as if it were either not very important or not very difficult, while we take for granted that every other job in our society that we believe is difficult *and* important relies on more than just instinct and love for success.

Fortunately, this is changing. More and more organizations are offering parenting courses, and more and more publishers are offering books about parenting. That's the good news. The bad news is that, with so much information coming out so quickly, parents are often overwhelmed trying to determine what is likely to be helpful and what isn't. A few key questions can help you make a quick and reasonable judgment:

1) Is the material based on a solid theory of child psychology?

2) Are the values it is based on consistent with life in a democratic society?

3) Are the skills practical, and are they presented with a lot of good examples?

4) Is the material interesting to read or watch?

Sometimes you have to begin reading to find the answers to these questions. Other times you can ask someone familiar with the material whose opinion you value. As for this book and my opinion, Julie Ross has superbly achieved all four goals. An accomplished Active Parenting group leader, she has done an excellent job applying a proven model of parent education to the specific needs of young children. Her underlying emphasis on respect for the child, coupled with an appreciation for the parent's role as leader in the family, form a useful foundation for the very practical skills and tips presented throughout the book. Her examples are charming, with a ring of truth that makes you want to say, "Yes, that's *my* child, too." Her analysis of each example not only serves to clarify the information, but also gives us parents, and even parent educators, permission to make mistakes.

And as the father of two young children, I know full well that parenting is too important and difficult to expect to do perfectly. Fortunately, mistakes *are* for learning, and this book will help.

Michael H. Popkin
Atlanta, 1993

I BELIEVE . . .

THE MYTH OF INSTINCTUAL PARENTING

I believe that being a parent is a difficult job that is underrated and undervalued. Some people, especially those hanging on to the threads of the "traditional American family," tend to slough off "parenting skills" as being instinctual. They deny the need for learned skills, claiming that, historically, parents have always relied on instinct, and children have not been harmed by this. The use of the word "instinct" implies not only an innate knowledge of how to care for your children, but also infers that "parental love" will guide the way in discipline, communication, and the relationship that you establish with your child. While this may sound idyllic to many parents, the good publicity that surrounds instinct and parental love has very little basis in historical fact.

In the eighteenth and early nineteenth centuries, for example, parental "instinct" allowed wakeful babies to be "knocked into the sleep of insensibility" through the "dumb, harmful custom of calming children with benumbing shaking and rocking." Likewise, parents would tightly swaddle their children, permitting them to "stew in their own excrement for hours on end." Parental instinct was also responsible for the practice of placing swaddled children close to the hearth to keep them warm, leaving them unattended, so that they perished when their swaddling clothes caught fire.[1]

"Parental love" has an equally questionable history. Today we seem to have romanticized the role that love played in parenting, when, in fact, parents of yesteryear looked upon children either indifferently or as a meal-ticket — someone in the family who would bring in extra money and share the burden of work, should they live to be old enough.[1]

While the emphasis placed on "bonding" by psychologists and doctors today has made great inroads into creating more loving parents, love can also be a wall behind which parents hide. Alice Miller states that, "Loving parents in particular should want to find out what they are unconsciously doing to their children. If they simply avoid the subject and instead point to their parental love, then they are not really concerned about their children's well-being but rather are painstakingly trying to keep a clear conscience."[2]

Parents who hide behind this wall of parental love and buy into the Myth of Instinctual Parenting are often unaware of what they are doing to their children in the name of instinct. In all likelihood, the "instinct" they are using is probably not based on genetic encoding passed down from one generation to the next, but rather is a result of their own early experiences as children, experiences that may have happened so early in life that they don't even consciously remember them.

If we believe that what we call instinct can solve the problems that we face as parents in today's complicated society, and if we believe that it can help us help our children solve the problems that they face, then we set ourselves up for failure. Within our own early and unremembered childhood, it is unlikely that our parents modeled the kind of skills we need to cope with the choices that children face today — choices about drug use, sex, and early independence, among others. In addition, because the experiences that we define as instinct happened so early in life that we have no conscious knowledge of them, we are risking our children's future based on subconscious feelings instead of facts.

Instinct will keep us forever searching for how to react if our child uses drugs, forever wondering where we went wrong if our child experiments with sex, forever reacting to life instead of acting on life. When we search for these hazy instincts within ourselves to help us solve the problems that arise in these challenging times, and come up blank or with solutions that don't work, we are then left with the belief that some flaw must exist in ourselves. The resulting feeling of helplessness comes from the knowledge that instinct can't be learned. This leaves us believing there is no way to change the feeling of inadequacy or solve the problem.

As parents, we need freedom from the Myth of Instinctual Parenting. We need it to free ourselves from feelings of helplessness and inadequacy, and we need it so that we don't risk our children's futures upon the forgotten events or habitual responses from our own childhood.

My name is Julie Ross, and I'm writing this book because I, too, bought into the Myth of Instinctual Parenting. Even though I held a Master's degree in Child Psychology at the time my daughter was born, some fundamental part of me believed that the minute I held my newborn in my arms, instinct would take over, and I would be able to understand and fulfill her needs.

In the following years, however, I learned that instinctual parenting is a myth. I have learned this through my own experience, as well as through the experiences of the parents I counsel and teach. The complex demands of society today make being a parent too risky to rely upon instinct. We educate ourselves for every other job we hold in society — being a parent shouldn't be the exception. Our children's futures are too important to leave to chance.

It is time to selectively integrate the wisdom and experience that our own parents, grandparents, and great grandparents have unknowingly passed on to us with the expertise of professional psychologists and parent educators, to create a synthesis of skills that can be used to supplement and strengthen the love we have for our children.

This book is a chronicle of my and other parents' experiences. It is filled with my own personal stories, as well as anecdotes told to me by the parents I teach and counsel. It is written with the hope that these examples will not only amuse, but also teach. And it is written with the hope that when you come to the end, you will take satisfaction in knowing that by being a parent, you hold the most important job in this country — one that requires a great deal of skill, and one in which you can take a great deal of pride.

As you step forward into the book, you will begin the most important journey that you will take as a parent — a journey into freedom from the Myth of Instinctual Parenting.

Julie A. Ross
New York City, 1993

"When we think about the well-being of our children, we plan to provide for them what was lacking for us. . . . Then, when the first child arrives we come face to face with the reality that parenting is much more than a loving dream. . . . Some days we find ourselves doing the very things we vowed we would never do. . . . Or we give in. . . . We need to learn skills, often many skills, that we did not learn in our families of origin."

— Jean Illsley Clarke and Connie Dawson[3]

ONE

LADYBUGS AND SPIDERS

LISTENING TO YOUR PREVERBAL CHILD: THE FIRST STEP IN GOOD COMMUNICATION

When my daughter, Emilie, was ten months old, we took her to a street fair — a unique phenomenon of spring and summer in New York, where thirty or more of the most well-traveled blocks are shut down for two whole weekend days, snarling traffic for miles, while jamming thousands of people shoulder to shoulder, so hundreds of chachka vendors can sell them things at exorbitant prices, which they never knew they wanted in the first place and will never use once they get them home.

We love street fairs.

Passing by a booth stocked with hand puppets, we decided that Emilie simply couldn't survive one more day without a puppet of her own. Two of the many choices caught our eyes: one was a spider, one a ladybug. In both cases, the puppeteer's hand fit into a glove, which then became the puppet's legs. The spider puppet was black, with yellow eyes and a penetrating stare. Its mouth was set in a grim straight line. The ladybug was red, with cute, curly antennae and a smile on its face. My husband, Steve, tried the spider puppet on first, manipulating the legs so that it "crawled" up my arm to my shoulders, where Emilie was perched. Her eyes widened, her mouth fell open, stark terror made her mute as she grabbed my hair and buried her face in it, trembling with fear.

We bought the ladybug.

The ladybug made her laugh. We felt that making her laugh was infinitely preferable to terrorizing her.

Though fear is one of the easier emotions to distinguish in a preverbal child, other emotions are subtler. Parents who "listen" carefully to their preverbal child in order to discover these feelings are parents who are laying the foundation for total communication with their child.

What *Is* Listening?

So how do you "listen" to a child who has no words? What does "listening" mean to someone who can't speak yet?

In order to answer those questions, we must recognize that listening is more than just *hearing* the person. Hearing occurs when sound waves enter the auditory canal and vibrate the tympanic membrane, causing it to . . . well, you get the picture. Hearing is a physical process.

Listening, on the other hand, is done with more than just our ears. Stephen R. Covey, in his book, *The 7 Habits of Highly Effective People*, says, "If I were to summarize in one sentence the single most important principle I have learned in the field of interpersonal relations, it would be this: Seek first to understand, then to be understood. [This ability] is absolutely critical . . ."[4]

True listening is more than just hearing. Listening means seeking to *understand* our children.

How Do We Listen?

So how do we do that?

Listening is made up of four things:

1) **Eye contact** — *watching* for emotions reflected in the child's face and body.

Using your eyes to listen is especially important when your child is an infant. Because infants can't verbalize their feelings, it is crucial that parents pay close attention to the child's facial expressions and body posture to determine how she's reacting to events around her. In the street fair scenario, our child didn't make a sound. But it was evident from her facial expression — wide eyes and open mouth — and from her physical reaction — grabbing my hair and burying her face — that she was very afraid.

2) **Body posture** on the part of the adult that conveys an attitude of receptiveness — either facing the child or bending down so that you're on the child's level. This helps the child feel they're being listened to.

3) **Verbal acknowledgment** on the part of the parent that they've "heard" their child — whether the child is verbal or not.

With a preverbal child, "verbal acknowledgment" might mean some guesswork on the part of the parent:

"Oh, Emilie, did you not want to see the puppet? Did it make you feel nervous?"

Verbal acknowledgment can also mean repetition. When a child is at the babbling stage, the parents can indicate they've "heard" their child by nodding their heads, repeating the infant's sounds, and making remarks along the lines of "Is that right?" followed by a repetition of the sounds. In other words, acting as though the child is actually speaking as an adult does.

While there are parents for whom this may feel uncomfortable, most parents do this naturally. The important point, however, is to convert that natural listening to a *conscious* decision. If parents consciously listen to their infant, and acknowledge to the infant that she is being heard, the infant will shortly begin to realize that the sounds she is making have an effect on the world. This is the beginning of creating a child who will use words ("I want that toy") instead of actions (throwing a tantrum, hitting) or screaming to get what she wants.

4) **Accepting the child's feelings** without trying to "fix" them or change them. This means allowing our children to feel the way they feel and empathizing with their feelings — even if those feelings are negative.

Though this last (and crucial) aspect of listening is more fully covered in Chapter Three, an illustration to clarify what I mean seems appropriate here.

How It Works

Two examples of how a parent could react to the street fair situation follow. One example illustrates a lack of acceptance of the child's feelings on the part of the parent, one indicates empathy. Pick out which is which:

The child has just widened her eyes and buried her head in her mother's hair. She is trembling with fear.

1) "Honey, are you scared? There's nothing to be afraid of. It's just a puppet. Sweetie, look. It's not scary, see?"

2) "Wow. That was really scary, huh? It really made you feel afraid."

While the loving tones of the first response seem to indicate that the parent has understood the child's fear, the parent has not followed through. By telling the child that the puppet is *not* scary, a message is given to her that her feelings are not valid. In other words, the parent is sending this message to her child: "I hear that you're afraid, but I don't understand why you'd feel that way." *Understanding our children means validating their feelings.*

The second response is better. Though not softened with terms of endearment, the message that the parent sends in the second response is far more validating. It says to the child, "I hear you. I understand that you're afraid. Being afraid is okay."

Fully listening and *realizing* that you're listening to your preverbal infant gives you the practice that you'll need to listen to your child when she becomes verbal. While it doesn't take much practice to recognize intense fear, there are more subtle emotions that take a great deal of practice to recognize, including feeling disappointed, feeling overwhelmed, feeling discouraged, feeling confident, and feeling confused, among others. Practicing your listening skills when your child is an infant will be to your advantage when the concepts that your child is experiencing and attempting to communicate are less than clear, as in the following example.

A Scary Mystery

When Joe and Patty's son, Billy, was fifteen months old, they took him to church with them. They sat down comfortably in the pew with Billy's aunt. Billy chose to stand just in front of the pew, in the little area where the kneelers are kept. Suddenly, he began backing up, making a loud, high pitched "ee, ee, ee" sound. His eyes were wide as saucers.

"Billy, shhh . . . what's wrong?"

(Notice that Patty fell first into denying or trying to quiet him down, and only after that did she actually ask him what was wrong. As I said, it takes a lot of practice.)

Billy scrambled up onto the pew, continuing what his parents considered odd and certainly disruptive behavior. Patty began to feel nervous about the noise he was making and almost told him that he could either be quiet or she'd take him out of the church, when Joe glanced at his son's face and caught sight of his eyes. Joe suddenly realized that Billy had never taken his eyes off something under the pew. Bending over, Joe realized that Billy's aunt had placed her large, black bag under the seat and that Billy was staring at it. It suddenly occurred to him that Billy might be afraid of the bag.

"Oh, Billy, are you nervous about this?" He pulled it out and showed it to him. "That must have seemed scary under the pew, where you didn't know what it was. Would you like to touch it? It's Aunt Catherine's purse."

Slowly, Billy's little hand went out, and he cautiously touched the bag. His body relaxed some, and it was evident that he was less fearful.

"See?" said Joe. "It's only a bag. It can't hurt you."

At that point, Billy's face relaxed, he calmed down and sat quietly for the rest of the service. Though to this day his parents don't know what he imagined the bag to be, judging from his actions, it must have been very scary!

While the emotion of fear was evident from the beginning, it would have been easy to remain ignorant of its cause. But by being used to listening to Billy with their eyes as well as their ears, and by knowing that, for a preverbal child, *watching* is the most important part of listening, Joe and Patty were able to determine what the problem was and help their son conquer his fear, and thus change his behavior.

Don't Forget Follow-Through

Joe and Patty also followed through by validating Billy's feelings. While they sought to educate him as to what the object was, they didn't deny his feelings of fear. Neither did they attempt to "fix" his feelings. Fortunately, showing him the bag did alleviate the problem. But had Billy still been afraid after the purse had been shown to him, Joe could have put the purse away, saying something to the effect of, "I can tell it still seems scary. I'll put it over here, where it won't bother you."

While both of the examples given in this chapter refer to fear, it's appropriate for parents to listen for other emotions as well. Infants have a wide variety of emotions — more than most parents give them credit for. Try watching your child and see if you can pick out some of the following emotions:

> Frustration
>
> Fear
>
> Amusement
>
> Accomplishment / Pride
>
> Satisfaction
>
> Anger
>
> Sadness

See if you can come up with some others that you've recognized your child experiencing.

Fostering the four aspects of listening within yourself — eye contact, body posture, verbal acknowledgment, and acceptance — will help you lay the foundation for the growth of your relationship with your child. And *recognizing* that you are actually listening to a preverbal child will cement that foundation together. When you accomplish this, you'll begin consciously moving toward a goal of fully understanding and communicating with your child.

TWO

"WHAT DID YOU SAY?"

MORE ABOUT LISTENING:
YOUR EARLY VERBAL CHILD

Many parents find that listening to their child gets easier as the child becomes more verbal. One thing is certain: it becomes more fun! Because children develop so quickly, however, it's often difficult to make the transition from non-verbal to "almost" or preverbal without a sense of awe. This astonishment at our children often results in an almost disbelieving response at their first use of words.

Sam told us this story about his daughter when she was just beginning to identify objects by name:

Pulling him by the hand, Sam's daughter Allison rushed down the hallway, pausing to place one hand on the closet door, where she looked up at him and said, "Door."

"What?" Sam asked.

"Door," she replied more emphatically than before.

"What, Allison?" he repeated, at which point, with a more than exasperated look in her eyes, she took her hand off the door, tugged her father's hand to continue walking and, in a very soft voice as they were leaving, repeated, "Door."

Sam laughed and said, "I could almost see Allison shaking her head in disbelief. What kind of father did she have anyway . . . certainly not one who would be her intellectual equal in later life!"

Begin With Repetition

It's often beneficial, when your child is just beginning to talk, to repeat the sounds, even if you don't understand them. In the example above, while it might not have given Sam immediate satisfaction and pride, had he repeated his daughter's sound without understanding it, *Allison* would have felt far more satisfied in the exchange.

Sam went on to say, "I didn't make this mistake only once. I eventually got into the habit of asking her to repeat *all* of her remarks. She must have either thought her father was dumb or hard of hearing, I don't know which!"

Sam eventually recognized this as a form of not listening and struggled to overcome his "What?" response and simply repeat her sounds, even though he didn't always understand immediately what it was she was referring to. This actually increased her production of words, in that she spent less time trying to make herself understood. It also made Sam a better listener and helped him figure out what Allison was saying.

As Sam grew used to "listening," he began to trust in Allison's ability to "speak," and the meaning would often become clear as they progressed through a "conversation":

Holding a toy elephant in her hand, Allison pointed to its trunk. "No!" she said.

"No!" Sam repeated, slightly puzzled.

Pointing to her own nose, Allison repeated, "No." Then, in rapid succession, leaving no doubt as to the meaning of her words, she pointed to the elephant's mouth and said, "Mou."

"Yes, Allison, yes!" Sam nodded his head enthusiastically, as pleased with himself for understanding her as with her correct identification of body parts. "That's right, mouth."

Of course, at that point, Allison calmly looked up at Sam with her big eyes, pointed to her ear and said, "Mou."

It Makes Sense — At Least To The Child

It took Sam awhile, but he was eventually able to trust that Allison was making sense — if not always to others, at least to herself. Trusting his daughter was the first step in helping her feel listened to, which in turn increased her confidence in producing words. Because he had faith in her, he was able to more fully acknowledge and empathize with her — even when he didn't completely understand her at first.

One mother's ability to trust her child resulted in a storytelling ability on the part of the child that far exceeded her developmental level. Cyndi related that while she didn't always understand the full meaning, she would acknowledge the fact that she was listening to her daughter, Jessica, with nods of her head and by focusing her full attention on her daughter. Thus, at age eighteen months, Jessica would tell whole stories about past events that went something like this:

"Ah ba dobar sah DOCTOR whinah mo do SLIDE ec foma me ah KNEE . . . AND *HURT*. Somah nana MOMMiDADDY an DOCTOR wenam a HURT!"

Cyndi related the details to our group: They had been playing on the slide at the park, and Jessica had hurt her knee badly enough to see a doctor. Mommy and Daddy had taken her to the doctor, and it proved to be a sprain. So even after she left the doctor's office, her knee still hurt.

Though Cyndi only clearly understood certain words within the story, her accepting attitude and clear acknowledgment that she knew Jessica was telling a story prompted the little girl to put her single words into storylike form, making her one jump ahead of others her age.

Trust — The Underlying Key

Trust your children. Respect their capabilities. These are principles that, if embraced, will fundamentally enhance all of the techniques and skills presented in this book. They will strengthen your communication with your child, provide encouragement, and build your children's confidence in themselves.

By trusting, we enable ourselves to listen. By listening, and by repeating and acknowledging our child's first verbal attempts, we begin to build upon the foundation we so carefully laid when our child was preverbal.

THREE

No Birds at the Zoo

Accepting Your Child's Feelings: The Next Step in Good Communication

You've learned from Chapter One that listening to your child with your eyes as well as your ears is crucial to facilitating good communication. The next step involves acknowledging the feelings you see or hear. Acknowledgment means more than just recognizing the feeling as being happy, sad, or angry. It involves something that is often very difficult for parents: stepping back and accepting how your child feels without trying to change it and without denying it.

Acknowledging Feelings

Paul and Lisa experienced how difficult it was to do this when Paul took their son, Ben, to the zoo. When Paul and Ben returned home, Lisa asked Ben if he had a good time.

"No," was his reply.

Paul looked surprised. "You didn't?" he asked.

"Of course, he did," Lisa said. "He always has a good time at the zoo. You had a good time, didn't you, Ben?"

"No!" he replied.

Paul looked disappointed, and Lisa turned to him. In an attempt to soothe his hurt feelings, she said, "Of course he did, honey. I know he did. Don't feel bad. He just doesn't understand what I'm asking." She then turned back to Ben and, assuming that it was all a misunderstanding, repeated herself: "Ben, did you have a good time at the zoo?"

"No, Mommy!" was the reply.

Finally, Lisa decided to try a different tact. "Why didn't you like the zoo, Ben?"

"No birds!" came his answer. Loud and clear. No birds.

Paul concurred — they hadn't seen birds at the zoo, and Ben had kept asking for them, but they just hadn't been out.

Lisa made a classic mistake in this situation: she tried to be the peacemaker, and in so doing, denied not only her child's feelings, but her husband's as well.

A Better Way

What could Lisa have done instead?

Perhaps the most obvious solution would have been to ask the question she finally did ask, but at the beginning of the exchange. Had she asked Ben *why* he didn't like the zoo, she would have saved her husband's feelings as well — both would have realized that Ben was simply disappointed at not having seen birds, and that his response had nothing to do with the interaction between his father and himself.

Sometimes, however, our own emotions are so tied up in the situation that it's difficult to detach ourselves enough to ask what would appear to be the obvious question. A useful approach in that case is simple repetition, for example, saying something along the lines of, "You didn't like the zoo this time." Ben may very well have replied then with the reason he didn't like it.

Why Our Attempts Don't Work

Parents often end up ignoring or denying their children's feelings because they are trying to avoid prolonging the emotional exchange. Many times, we try to distract our child in an attempt to "take his mind off it." Other times, parents will try to reason with the child, believing that logic will prevail, and once he sees how "illogical" he's being, he will calm down.

Unfortunately, reasoning with children doesn't work. Children cannot reason in the same way that adults can — they are not capable of using the same type of processes that adults use. When an adult attempts to reason a child out of his feelings, it often has the opposite effect of what the parent intends — it prolongs the experience rather than shortening it.

An experience that I had dramatically illustrates this point.

Reflection, Not Reasoning

I was at a small gathering at a friend's home where several children were present. One of them, Kristi, who was three years old at the time, was watching a video on the TV. She was sitting next to her mother, Monica, who was busy talking to one of the adults. I was sitting on the other side of Kristi. She watched the video with rapt attention, her eyes never straying from the screen, even though the room was filled with conversation.

When the video ended, Kristi turned to her mother. "More, Mommy. More video," she said emphatically.

Monica turned to her. "It's over, honey. There is no more."

Kristi's voice raised. "Want more! More video," she shouted angrily.

"That was the end, Kristi. When it's over, it's over."

Kristi turned her face to the couch. Angry tears began to roll down her face. She grabbed a pillow and began to hit the couch with it. "More, more, more!" she yelled. I could tell that her mother was beginning to feel nervous about the yelling — people were beginning to stop their conversations and look in our direction.

I leaned over to Kristi and, in a quiet voice, said, "Boy, you feel really angry that the tape is over."

Kristi stopped pounding the pillow and looked at me. "Yeah!" she said.

"It's hard when you're enjoying something and it ends. You feel angry when that happens."

Kristi straightened up and wiped the tears off her face with the back of her hand. "Yeah," she said again, and walked quietly away.

This story illustrates how dramatically a child will change from tearful and angry, to calm and "reasonable," if they simply feel listened to. Monica's attempt to repeatedly "explain" that the tape was over merely prolonged the episode. So, in addition to Kristi not getting what she wanted, she also felt misunderstood.

Parental attempts to take "shortcuts" through distraction or reasoning often result in *both* sides feeling misunderstood, which only extends this type of angry exchange.

Take The Good With The Bad

While this chapter deals mainly with acknowledging our children's *negative* feelings and statements, it's just as important that we acknowledge our children's *positive* feelings. Actually, most parents naturally find it easier when the feelings are "good" rather than "bad."

For example, when your child comes home with an "A" on her math test, has a smile on her face, and is shouting for you to come look, it's easy to say, "Wow, you must be so excited! Good job!" Most parents don't necessarily need practice acknowledging their children's feelings when the feelings are pleasant. There is more immediacy to the payoff they receive when they acknowledge positive feelings — they get to share the experience with their child. But what parent wants to share a negative experience? Not many, I'd say. Yet the payoff is just as large, if not larger — it's simply delayed.

Positive Payoffs

What is the payoff for sharing a negative experience? The payoff is that you will establish a deeper, more communicative relationship with your child. You'll help your child learn to label her internal states — she will use words to describe how she's feeling instead of acting out. She will feel understood by you and seek your advice and counsel when she's going through a difficult time. You will, in essence, say to your child, "I don't just love and understand you when you're happy. My love is deeper than that. I love you all the time. I'm here for you, even (or especially) when you're upset or angry. Even if that anger is directed at me."

This is a large payoff indeed. But because it's a large payoff, it takes more of an investment. You must be willing to take a deep breath sometimes and put aside your own anger ("How dare you talk to me that way"), embarrassment ("What are people thinking when my child acts this way?"), and other negative emotions, and acknowledge and accept your child's feelings *in spite of what you are feeling*. Not easy, but certainly worth it in the end.

Practice, Practice, Practice

Accepting your child's feelings — especially the negative ones — is probably the most difficult step in good communication. Begin practicing now. When your son says, "I hate my brother!", instead of saying, "That's not nice. You should love your brother," say, "You must feel really angry at him right now." When your daughter says, "I'm never going to school again!", instead of saying, "What are you talking about? You have to go to school," say, "Sounds like you're upset over something that happened. Would you like to talk about it?"

And don't stop with your children. After all, practice makes perfect. So practice with your spouse as well. When she says, "My boss is a pig. I can't stand that job anymore," instead of saying, "Honey, you know we need your income to pay for the kids' education," say, "You must have had a tough day. Let's talk." When he says, "The kids are driving me crazy. This place is a mess," instead of saying, "I don't think it's so bad. Just tell them to pick up their stuff," say, "It's hard when the kids make a mess like this. It can really get on your nerves."

And practice with your preverbal, two-week-old infant. When she's crying because she's hungry, instead of saying, "I'm coming, I'm coming," say, "It's hard to wait when you're so hungry, isn't it?" When he's cranky because his diaper is wet, instead of saying nothing and simply changing the diaper, say, "It sure is uncomfortable to have a wet diaper, isn't it?"

Practice, practice, practice. Practice so that you can be the kind of parent your child will want to talk to — even when she has something negative to say.

FOUR

CHASING OUR CHILDREN

KEEPING UP WITH YOUR
CHILD'S DEVELOPMENT

Children develop quickly, and as parents, we're often trying to "catch up" with them. Many times, we don't realize that our children are light-years ahead of where we think they are.

Long before a child is able to articulate words, and long before she will be able to communicate all her needs to her parents, the child is absorbing information, processing it, and committing it to long-term memory. In short, the child is *understanding* the information that is available to her.

Many parents, however, make the assumption that if a child doesn't indicate that she understands, she must not be taking in the information. They are continually waiting for that outward sign of the internal process. Unfortunately, they could wait forever. By the time the child can articulate understanding, she has also grasped that it may be to her advantage *not* to understand, and she may use that piece of information wisely.

Acceptance vs. Expectation

There is, perhaps, a fine balance between accepting our child at any particular stage of development, while at the same time keeping our expectations positive. But like any of the balancing acts that we must accomplish as parents, the payoff is great. Positive expectations about our children's capabilities (in this case, their ability to understand what's being said to them or required of them) will set up patterns of communication that will continue throughout their lifetimes. Likewise, negative expectations will result in a chase in which we may never catch up with them.

When Should You Begin To Set Limits?

Rebecca, who had already taken my Active Parenting[5] class and was now in a support group, related that she had recently been talking to a mother who had a two-year-old boy. Their conversation was extremely fragmented, because the boy kept running off, and his mother (seven months pregnant with her second at the time) would literally have to run after him. In between episodes of chasing, she noticed that Rebecca was not having a similar problem with her son, Kenny. Though extremely active, Kenny listened well if Rebecca asked him to stop what he was doing and always asked before leaving the picnic blanket. The other mother attributed this behavior to Kenny being a year older than her son.

"Actually," Rebecca explained, "from the time Kenny was an infant, we taught him what the limits were, and we've been quite consistent about enforcing them. Because he was in my office with me full-time almost from birth, we felt it was essential that he be given limits — if for no other reason than to protect him from danger. The limits and our method of communicating those limits are what make him a good listener."

"But how did you give him those limits?" the mother queried.

"Well, I learned a technique called Active Parenting," Rebecca replied. "Kenny has grown up with my husband and myself consistently utilizing its principles."

"What do you do?" asked the other mother.

Rebecca smiled. "It's a bit difficult to explain in a short period of time, but I'll try to summarize it for you. First you give the child what's called an 'I' message.

"'I' messages are very short statements that tell the child what behavior isn't acceptable, how you feel about the behavior and why, and what you want him to do differently. Then, if he doesn't respond to the 'I' message, you give him a choice with a consequence — for example, if you wanted to give a choice to your son about his running off, you might tell him that he can either sit with you on the blanket or sit in his stroller.

"It's a way of giving your child some power without giving up your own power as the parent." (Setting limits with "I" messages and consequences is covered more fully in Chapters Six and Seven.)

"Oh," said the Mom, looking tired. "Well, my husband and I agree that we'll start reasoning with him as soon as he can understand us. We really believe in reasoning, but right now he's still too little to understand."

And then she was off and running again, trying to catch up — in more ways than one — with her bright two-year-old son.

When *Do* They Understand?

As Rebecca told this story to our group, she wondered aloud about what criteria that other mother would be using to determine that her child understood. What constitutes understanding? At what age does a child "understand?" If not at two years old, then when?

Child development specialists can make some pretty good guesses as to when children begin to understand the various pieces of information that are presented to them. But, like parents, they are dependent upon outward signs to "prove" that internal process. Therefore, rather than giving you ages at which children "understand" certain things, I would like to suggest that, for practical purposes, you should assume that your child "understands" from birth. This doesn't mean that you should expect them to pick up their toys at three months old because you've told them to. It does mean that you should practice the skills and techniques presented in this book *without expecting results* from the time your child is born. Talking to and behaving towards your child as if he understands will promote understanding, set up good listening habits, and most of all, give *you* practice!

How Will I *Know* They Understand?

I know, your next question is, "But when *can* I expect results?"

The answer is this — if you begin these techniques when your child is an infant, you can expect results the minute your child *does* begin to understand you.

If you are reading this book and your child is past infancy, but not quite old enough for you to be sure that he understands — don't despair! By beginning these techniques now, *following through* with them in a consistent manner, and watching your child closely, it will be quite evident when your child begins to understand. With these techniques, there is very little guesswork involved in knowing whether your child is understanding you. But it will require patience on your part — repeating the skills over and over, even when you're *sure* your child isn't getting it.

If your child is two years or older, simply be assured that he does indeed understand and carry on.

Negative Expectations — One Year Later

But what happens when a parent does *not* expect their child to understand? In other words, what happened to the woman in the story that Rebecca told us?

Well, a year later, Rebecca said that she had run into this same mother. Now her son was the same age that Rebecca's son, Kenny, had been the first time they met. The support group was curious about whether the child was a better listener now that he was a year older. The look on Rebecca's face told all.

Unfortunately, and perhaps predictably, the child had not changed. He didn't listen any better at age three than he had at age two. It was clear that his mother was *still* waiting for him to understand.

When we expect our children not to understand, we can be assured that they won't — children live up to our negative expectations just as easily as they do to our positive ones.

Positive Expectations

So what do we do about that? How can we change our negative expectations into positive ones?

Positive expectations are simply a matter of perspective, much like the optical illusion (shown opposite) that, at first glance, appears to be the portrait of an old and ugly woman. With a bit of concentration and a shift in focus, though, it is seen as a very beautiful, young woman. But it's difficult, if not impossible, to see both portraits at the same time. We choose what to see. Old and ugly versus young and beautiful. Likewise, in our lives, we choose to focus on the negative or the positive. It's difficult to focus on both at the same time.

Having positive expectations for your child is a matter of saying to yourself, "I will tell him this because he does understand." (Don't forget — if he doesn't understand, you're at least getting practice, so that the minute he does, you're already used to communicating with him.)

Something New Every Day

Another benefit to having positive expectations for our children is that it allows us to better prepare them for the new situations that they face every day.

Helping our children face new, unknown, or unexpected situations is extremely important. Children worry about the unknown or unexpected, just as many adults do. With children, however, *most* of the events in their lives are unknown or unexpected, since they have so little world experience. By expecting that our children are constantly absorbing information, we can ease their growth, helping them to face the challenges of life more effectively and courageously.

When Elizabeth's daughter, Samantha, was fifteen months old, they had to visit the doctor for a post-ear infection check up. While Samantha was very content in the waiting area, the mere

(Hint: To see the young woman, focus on the upper part of the image. To see the old woman, focus on the lower part.)

sight of the doctor caused her to burst into tears.

It took Elizabeth a few moments to realize that Samantha was remembering the doctor's visit of two weeks before, when the doctor had looked into her ears and it had been very painful. Elizabeth had fallen into the trap most parents do — not giving her child credit for understanding and remembering.

Had Elizabeth realized that her daughter might remember the person who had caused her pain before, she might have been able to better prepare her for the visit:

"Samantha, we're going to the doctor today. She's going to look in your ears. Can you show me your ears? Last time we went, it might have hurt. This time, you've been taking medicine, and it's not going to hurt this time, because you're all better."

Or she might have shown her a book with pictures of children at the doctor. Or purchased a toy medical bag and played doctor. Samantha could have looked in her mother's ears or her teddy bear's ears.

Giving Due Credit

Elizabeth might have made the visit easier — *had she recognized and given Samantha credit for her ability to understand.* In other words, had she *respected* Samantha's capabilities.

I don't think any parent starts out intending to be disrespectful of their children's capabilities. I believe it comes from not remembering how difficult and challenging childhood is. Most parents don't realize how much their children are accomplishing — from the minute they're born. And without that realization, it's difficult to take the next step and respect our children's knowledge, understanding, and cognitive capabilities.

Acknowledging Accomplishments

In order to respect our children's intelligence, we must first acknowledge their past accomplishments and not take those accomplishments for granted.

It was at a church picnic, when my daughter, Emilie, was almost a year old, that I was talking to two other mothers. One had an eight-year-old boy, Kevin, the other an eight-month-old boy, Andrew. We were talking about the meaning of certain names. One of those names happened to be "Emily." It was mentioned that "Emily" means "industrious, hard worker."

Kevin's mother said, "Well, Julie has an Emilie, but it remains to be seen whether she will be a hard worker and industrious."

"Are you kidding?" I said. "Emilie is a very hard worker."

"Yeah," said Andrew's mother (who, by the way, was looking a bit haggard at the moment). "Emilie and Andrew work hard at playing. That's about all."

I'm afraid that was all it took to get me on my soapbox. "Wait a moment," I said. "Have you ever thought about how hard it would be if you had to learn to walk again? Not to mention the things our children have already accomplished, like sitting, crawling, and standing. And the things they still have to achieve, like learning the English language? I think they work very hard. Imagine if you were suddenly disabled and had to learn all those things again. It would be very hard work."

Andrew's mother looked pensive. "Hmm. I never thought of that before," she said. "That's a good way to look at it."

I believe that it's the *only* way to look at it.

Children Deserve Respect

If we belittle our children's greatest achievements, we're not building the kind of foundation on which respect can flourish. And if we don't respect their accomplishments and their ability to understand and make sense of the world, we cannot adequately prepare them to face life, with all its limits, challenges, and surprises.

Without that fundamental sense of respect, we essentially relegate our children to the level of most animals, who understand only the most basic commands.

And most important, if we fail to recognize that our children are capable of understanding the world, and if we belittle their successes, what will that do to their sense of self? How will they feel about all their other accomplishments later?

We *must* have positive expectations.

We *must* respect our children's accomplishments.

We *must* acknowledge our children's increasing capabilities.

These basic convictions will pave the road for us as parents — in our communication, our discipline, and fundamentally, in our whole relationship with our children. With these attitudes under our belts, we won't spend the rest of our lives running after our children, always trying to "catch up."

FIVE

THE MIXED VEGGIE PHENOMENON

LIFE'S VALUABLE LESSONS

Parents can give themselves a much-deserved break from the responsibility of teaching their children by taking advantage of what I call the "Mixed Veggie Phenomenon" — allowing life to be our children's teacher. It involves standing back at certain times and giving our children the chance to learn from the natural lessons that life offers, without rushing in and "making it all better" or getting into power struggles. I call it the Mixed Veggie Phenomenon because of the following story:

Rhonda's daughter, Susan, age two-and-a-half, had been served a plate of mixed vegetables for dinner.

"MommiDaddy?" Susan looked at her parents imploringly. "I want that stuff."

"That stuff" happened to be popcorn seasoning — a blend of salt and "butter flavoring."

"Okay, honey," said Rick, her father, "I'll put it on for you."

"No, no, no! I put it on!!"

About to reject this kind, but impractical offer, Rick stopped and thought a moment, then decided to give Susan a chance to try herself. He handed the seasoning to her, cautioning as he did so: "It comes out fast, Susie, so shake it slowly and carefully. If you put too much on it won't taste good."

Susan began putting the seasoning on her vegetables and quickly got carried away, saturating them with the salty mixture. When the veggies were covered with yellow seasoning, she triumphantly handed it back to her father, proudly proclaiming, "Done!"

Rick, to his credit, allowed the lesson to continue. Picking up a spoon, Susan shoveled a large mouthful of vegetables into her mouth. Her parents reported that the look on her face was unlike anything they'd ever seen before — distorted and horrified. Then she burst into tears.

Helping It Along

At this point, many parents would have either laughed or rushed in to "make it all better," getting her a drink of water or fixing a second plate of vegetables.

Susie's Mom and Dad did neither. Instead, they strengthened the lesson of the mixed veggies by remaining calm, yet sympathetic, and by helping Susie work out a solution to her problem by herself:

"Oh, dear," said her mother, Rhonda. "It looks like that tasted terrible. Can we do anything to help?"

"Water," Susie blubbered through her tears.

Rick handed her a glass of water, which she promptly drank. She looked down at her plate again, and seeing the mountain of seasoning, burst into fresh tears.

Rhonda took the cue from her and said, "Uh-oh, it's still on your dinner. I wonder if you can think of anything that we can do about that."

The sobs lessened somewhat, being replaced by hiccoughing.

Susie looked again at the plate, as Rick and Rhonda waited patiently. After a short period of silence, Susie replied, "Wash?"

"Great idea, honey," said Rick. "I'll wash them off for you."

Compassion and Support

Rick and Rhonda handled this beautifully. They not only allowed life to be Susie's teacher, but they reinforced the lesson gently while not taking over and fixing the problem. Instead, they supported Susie in finding her own solution. Though Susie was only two-and-a-half at the time, she not only learned a valuable lesson, but also something about problem solving.

The Rules

There are a few points that parents should keep in mind when taking advantage of the Mixed Veggie Phenomenon:

1) If the lesson that life might teach your child could *in any way* be dangerous, by all means, STEP IN! Don't allow your child to learn from experience if it might injure her or endanger her life.

2) Remember that there must be a direct and fairly immediate connection between your child's action and the lesson or consequence. If there is too much time in between, no lesson will be learned. For example, telling a child not to eat candy because she'll get cavities is too remote to make an impression.

3) One swift and sure way to *ruin* your child's lesson is to say, "I told you so." Be careful of this — the "I told you so" monster can creep in without you even knowing it, and many parents think they are reinforcing the lesson, when in reality they are actually spoiling it. "I told you so" only humiliates the child and makes her feel defiant.

4) Genuine sympathy for your child's predicament will reinforce

the lesson and set you up in a position of support. Note that Rhonda and Rick took the cue for being sympathetic from the look on Susie's face, not from their own knowledge that the vegetables would taste terrible. They said, "It *looks like* that tasted terrible," not "I *knew* too much seasoning wouldn't taste good" or "I told you not to put too much on." Thus, instead of setting themselves up as know-it-all's and people to defy, they took the opportunity to be Susie's support system — people to be relied upon, trusted, and ultimately respected.

5) If you support your child in coming up with her own solution to the problem, you will have run the lesson home as no "I told you so" could ever have done. In addition, you will have started your child on the road to seeking solutions for the problems that life will present to her, as well as giving her the ability to solve problems of her own creation. Rick and Rhonda did this by saying, "Can we do anything to help?" and "I wonder if you can think of anything that we can do about that?"

Sometimes the child will not be able to come up with a solution as Susie did. At that point the parents can present solutions they may have thought of. As long as they show some hesitancy in presenting their own solutions and allow *the child* to make the choice, it won't come across as if they are know-it-alls. For example, Susie's parents could have said, "I wonder what would happen if we washed them off — would they taste better then? Do you think that would help?"

6) Finally, Rick and Rhonda achieved the crowning glory in this scene when, at the end, they said, "Great idea, honey!" when Susie asked about washing the vegetables. This final encouraging statement gave Susie the credit she deserved for being able to think clearly and come up with a solution (even though they helped). In so doing, her parents focused on the *lesson* that life taught her, not on the original mistake she made. And they did so by building her self-esteem, not by putting themselves in a position of authority.

SIX

"HE BIT ME!"

THE BEGINNING OF DISCIPLINE

A mother in one of my classes shared this problem with us:

"It's about biting," she said. "My fourteen-month-old son gets so enthusiastic and excited sometimes that he bites. It hurts, but I think he's just being playful and doesn't know his own strength. I don't want to punish him for it, since he's doing it so good-naturedly. What should I do?"

Biting, hitting, pinching, and kicking are common problems that almost every parent experiences at one point or another. Sometimes they occur in play, as in the above scenario, and sometimes in anger. As parents, we're more likely to allow these behaviors if they're being done good-naturedly, in a playful way. But allowing physical aggression towards another person to continue unchecked for *any* reason is harmful. As I told this mother, "People are not for biting. Or hitting, or kicking, should it come up. People are for hugging and kissing and being gentle with. It's okay to engage in rough-and-tumble play with your child, playfully wrestling or bouncing. But when the behavior gets out of hand and it could really hurt someone, that's where you must draw the line."

Punishment vs. Discipline

"But what should I do?" questioned the mother. "He's so happy when he's doing it, I feel that if I punish him, he'll think I'm punishing him for being happy."

The key is not in punishment, but in discipline.

What's the difference? Well, punishment is based on the philosophy that you must hurt your child (verbally or physically) in order to teach him not to behave a certain way. Sometimes parents punish by spanking, sometimes by yelling, sometimes by isolating their child or withdrawing their love by not speaking to him for a period of time. All of these things hurt the child, either physically or psychologically. But if you're trying to teach your child *not* to hurt *you*, what will hurting *him* accomplish? Remember that our children learn how to behave by watching and imitating us. If we hurt our children, no matter how lofty our goals, we teach them how to hurt us (and others) as well.

How Do I Know If My Discipline Is Working?

I like to give parents two guidelines that are extremely useful in measuring how effective our discipline is with our children. I tell parents, whenever you discipline your child, ask yourself these two questions:

1) Is the discipline working? (Has it changed my child's behavior in a positive way?)

2) What am I teaching my child? What values am I expressing about the way people treat each other? What am I teaching him about how to get people to do what he wants?

Punishment — yelling, spanking, belittling, isolating — may work. It may change your child's behavior. But what does it teach your child about the way people should treat each other? Most often, it teaches a child that if you are bigger, stronger, or in authority, you have the right to belittle, yell, hurt, or hit someone else when you want to get your way. Ultimately, it doesn't satisfy the second guideline for effective discipline.

What Can I Do Instead?

So, you may be asking yourself, what do you mean by discipline? What do I do instead of punishing my child? What technique will satisfy *both* requirements for effective discipline?

As you progress through this book, you will find many valuable tools for handling the specific problems that may come up with your child. All of these tools satisfy both of the above requirements, and all are based on a concept that may or may not be new to you when you think of your relationship with your child — the concept of respect. By respecting our children, we will not only gain their respect, but ensure that the tools we use work to their maximum efficiency.

R-E-S-P-E-C-T

If you're not sure you're being respectful to your child, ask yourself these questions:

1) Would I treat my spouse this way?

2) Would I treat my best friend this way?

3) Would I want to be treated this way?

If the answer is "no," you're not being respectful to your child, and the discipline tools you're using won't be as effective, and might even cause your child to rebel.

"But what do I do?" you might be thinking. "It's easy to be respectful to my spouse and friends. They don't bite! Tell me the discipline tools for handling biting, kicking, or hitting. Let me *see* the difference between discipline and punishment."

Before I do, let me say that it *is* easier to respect someone who doesn't bite you. But your family and friends have already learned not to bite. Your job, as the parent, is to lovingly teach your child which behaviors are appropriate and which are inappropriate. Discipline is the way in which you do that teaching. Because discipline focuses on the *behavior,* and not the child, it's more respectful by nature. Punishment, which is disrespectful by nature, attacks the *person* rather than the behavior.

The "I" Message

One of the most effective disciplinary tools is called the "I" message. This tool can be used whenever you feel upset or concerned about something your child is doing.

In one of my classes, there was a father whose wife had attended the previous semester. When we completed the session on "I" messages and I was about to dismiss the class, I asked if there were any questions or comments. He bravely raised his hand and confessed, "When my wife came home from your class last semester and talked about 'I' messages, I thought she meant 'E-Y-E' messages. I thought it was some kind of eye contact, or that she was giving my son 'the eye.' I could tell it was working, because his behavior changed for the better, but I never could figure out what kind of look she was giving my son that made the difference. Thanks for clarifying."

So, if an "I" message isn't an "eye" message, what is it?

What It Is

The "I" message is a concise verbal statement that tells your child how you feel about his behavior. It gives him an explanation of the situation, how you believe it's going wrong, and what you want done differently.

WHAT IT IS NOT

It is *not* allowing your child to get away with unacceptable behavior while you talk and don't act.

THE FORM

"I" messages exist in several different forms. Some of the literature suggests simply stating to your child how you feel. In other words, "I feel angry about biting." Other authors suggest a two-fold "I" message, containing feelings and a suggested change for the child. For example, "I feel angry. I want you to stop biting." The "I" message that I prefer includes four distinct parts, and is borrowed from Michael Popkin's Active Parenting workshop and book.[5,6] It looks like this (the four distinct parts are underlined):

> "When you bite, I feel angry, because it hurts.
> I would like you to hug me instead."

By including the **misbehavior** of the child, your **feelings** about the behavior and **why** you feel that way, as well as telling the child **what you specifically want him to do differently**, you provide him with all the information he needs to change his misbehavior into acceptable behavior. That doesn't necessarily mean that his behavior *will* change — sometimes you'll have to follow up your "I" message with an action, as you'll see later in this book — but many times the "I" message works all by itself.

In the chapters that follow, you'll see this specific format for "I" messages used again and again. You'll see how it's applied in various situations that arise with our children, and you'll read stories confirming the best part of all — IT WORKS!

Why The "I" Message Works

There are several reasons why the "I" message works that are relevant to this discussion:

1) It's non-threatening — it doesn't attack the child, only his behavior, which keeps him from getting defensive.

2) Because the parent actually memorizes lines, much like an actor does, it allows the parent to remain calm. A calm parent is more resourceful and less likely to resort to hurting the child, either with words or actions.

3) It forces the parent to be very specific about what s/he wants the child to do differently. Many times, parents assume that a child knows how to change his behavior without being told. But children are inexperienced, and they can't read minds. They need their parents to be clear about what appropriate behavior is. In addition, children want to know what the rules are — it helps them to feel that their parents are in control and that they are safe.

Whenever I teach this technique, I always send the parents out of the class with the words, "Try it! You might be surprised how well it works!" Most parents leave with doubt written all over their faces, and I can tell that they're thinking, "How on earth could mere words work, when I've been yelling and screaming and punishing and none of that worked?"

Inevitably, they come back the next week and the doubt has been replaced by astonishment. One father told this story:

The "I" Message In Action

"I can't believe it! I have an incredible story to tell you! My wife went away on a business trip, and when she returned, she brought home some necklaces for our two-year-old daughter. Jenny was really excited to see her Mom and get the presents. She immediately draped all of the necklaces around her neck and began to jump on the bed. Now, we don't care if she jumps on the bed as long as we're with her, but I felt concerned that the necklaces might choke her if they got tangled up. I started to speak harshly and demand that she get off the bed, but then I decided to try out the 'I' message instead. I said 'Jenny, when you jump on the bed with the necklaces on, I feel nervous, because they might get tangled and hurt you. I would like you to stop jumping on the bed when you're wearing the necklaces.' And you know what my daughter said? She said, 'Okay, Daddy,' and got right off! It worked!"

When parents try the "I" message after months of nagging, yelling, or spanking, they are invariably amazed at how powerful it is. Once our children no longer feel as though their self-esteem is being threatened, and they're clear on what we'd like them to do, they react much more positively to our corrections.

What If It Doesn't Work?

What about the Mom who was faced with a child who bit her? Did the "I" message work with her as well? The answer is "yes," but she had to pair it with an action first. Once her child discovered that after Mom gave the "I" message she would act, he eventually stopped biting because of the "I" message alone. (See Chapter Seven for more about the action following the "I" message.) Let me tell you how that story ends:

ADDING AN ACTION

I told the mother to begin by giving her child an "I" message. When she returned the next week, she reported that although her child stopped the first time she tried it, the very next day, he was gleefully biting again and ignoring her. I suggested that the next time he bit her, she should give an "I" message, and when he bit her again, she should give him this choice: "Either stop biting, or I'll go into the other room." Then, if he did it again, she should immediately leave the room and tell him he'd have a chance to try again later. Should he follow her, I suggested she keep her back turned for a specific amount of time, reinforcing her action by saying that she doesn't stay around people who bite, and he'd have another chance in two minutes. She agreed to try this.

The following week she returned, shaking her head woefully. "It didn't work," she proclaimed sadly. "He was very upset when I left the room, and he cried. You see? It didn't work!"

"Wait a second — tell me the story," I suggested. "Maybe I can figure out what happened."

"Well, I did what you said. I gave him the 'I' message, and he bit me again. So I gave him the choice, and he still bit me, so I left the room. He cried the whole two minutes until I came back."

I asked, "When you came back, did he bite you again?"

"Well, no," she said. "But he was so unhappy when I left."

"Has he bitten you since?"

"No."

"Sounds to *me* like it worked!" I replied.

"But he was so sad. I stopped him from doing something he enjoyed and made him sad."

"But it worked!" I emphasized. "And just because a particular misbehavior makes our children happy, that doesn't mean we should tolerate it. What you did worked. Give yourself credit. You put a limit on your child that will not only improve his relationship with you, but also with his peers. No one, not even another child, wants to be around a kid who bites."

Give Yourself Credit

It's important to recognize when the techniques we use are working. A lot of parents who try these techniques will, at first, credit the disappearance of their children's misbehavior to it having been a stage or a process of natural extinction. *Recognize* when you're having an effect on your child, and you'll be more capable of duplicating that effect at another time.

Also, realize that while your child may cry or act unhappy about the limits you place on his behavior, it's your job as the adult to keep the bigger picture in mind. In the case of the biting child, the picture had to include an awareness that people are not made to be bitten, and that it's socially inappropriate and harmful — not only to the person being bitten, but to the child's future relationships as well.

As you begin to try the techniques set forth throughout this book, remember to encourage yourself. Give credit where credit is due. And as your child's misbehavior lessens, when someone says to you, "Aren't you lucky, you have such a good child," you can reply with confidence, "Luck has nothing to do with it!"

SEVEN

"Why Did You Stop the Car?"

Acting After the "I" Message: Coming Up With Creative Choices

"I" messages work. Sometimes. So what happens when they don't work? What's the next step in teaching our children about appropriate behavior?

The next step in disciplining our children — in other words, teaching them which behaviors are appropriate and which are not — involves choices.

Throughout our lives as adults, we are constantly faced with choices. We must decide everything from what clothes to buy and wear, to where we want to live, to what we want to do with our lives. Some people seem to make great choices all the time. Some people make terrible choices — often leading to disaster. Most of us make a mixture of choices — some good, some not so good.

Making Choices

What governs our decisions? What is the factor that leads us to choose one thing over another? And why does it seem that some people make great choices — at least most of the time?

The factor that governs the choices we make is called **consequences**.

In order to make a choice about anything, we must first ask ourselves, "What do I ultimately want to happen? What outcome do I want from this choice?" When we know the outcome (or consequence) of each of our choices, we are then capable of choosing one over another. People who seem to make "great" choices most of the time are generally those people who carefully think through the consequences of each of their options before deciding.

We have choices about everything we do in life. Sometimes we don't acknowledge those choices, but nevertheless, they exist. For example, when we stand at a street corner and the light is red, most of us assume we have no choice — we stand there instead of crossing so that we don't get hit by a car. In actuality, however, we *are* making a choice. The other option is to cross against the red, the consequence of which would be risking our lives. Because the consequence of this choice is so blatant, though, we tend not to see it as a choice at all.

The first step in making good choices is to recognize that we *have* choices about *everything*. Some choices are more obvious and the consequences more disastrous than others, but the choice *still exists*. Becoming aware of all of our options and their accompanying consequences will lead us to make better choices.

Learning To Make Choices

There are two ways to teach our children how to make better choices. The first is by example. By thinking through the consequences of the options that we face as parents, and making our decisions based on the outcome we want to achieve, our children will see adults who act responsibly, not on impulse.

The second way to teach our children how to *make* better choices is by *giving* them choices and enforcing the consequences of their choices in a clear and deliberate manner. This is also the second step in disciplining our children — what you will use when "I" messages don't work.

Following Choice With Action

In a workshop I was teaching, a father spoke up. "I've got an impossible problem," he said. "My two-year-old has to sit in a car seat whenever we drive somewhere, and he hates it. From the minute he's in it until the minute he gets out, he screams. And the worst thing is, we're usually going somewhere that he enjoys — like the zoo. He still screams, even when I tell him we have to drive to get there. It's very hard to concentrate on driving when he's screaming like that."

I told the father to give his son an "I" message:

"When you scream, I feel nervous, because I can't concentrate on driving. I would like you to play quietly with your toys when we're in the car."

"He won't even hear it," the father exclaimed. "That's how loud he is. You see what a problem this is?"

"Give the 'I' message anyway," I explained, "because even if you believe he can't hear the meaning, he can hear that you're saying something. The next step will be to give him a choice, and by pairing the 'I' message with the choice/consequence combination that you'll set up, he'll eventually learn to stop his behavior with the 'I' message alone. That's why you always give an 'I' message first."

"Next, you'll give him a choice. Right now, he's making the choice to scream. But there are no consequences to his screaming, except the ones that *you're* suffering. Let's set it up so that the choice you ask him to make involves consequences that *he* has to live with. For example, you might say 'Either play quietly with your toys when we're in the car, or we won't go to the zoo.' Then, if he continues to scream, turn the car around and go straight home."

The father looked thoughtful. "That might work," he said. "But that would get him out of the car seat, which is what he wants. He has to learn how to ride in the car seat. Also, what about if we're meeting his friend there or something. I mean, what if we have to keep going and can't turn around and go back for some reason?"

"Then you might want to make the choice more along the lines of, 'Either play quietly with your toys when we're in the car, or I'll stop the car until you choose to be calm'."

"Yeah!" the father began to get excited. "And that would also mean he'd still have to stay in his car seat. His screaming wouldn't get him out of what he hates. Instead, the consequence of his screaming would be that he doesn't get where he wants to go as quickly."

Another parent spoke up. "But what if you're going somewhere in a hurry? Stopping the car could take a lot of time, and you'd be late. Also, should he pull over right away, on the shoulder of the highway?"

"No, pull *off* the highway. Look for the next rest stop. Find a safe parking lot. It's dangerous to stop on the shoulder of the road. You can take the extra time it requires to find a safe spot, and the consequence will still be effective."

Take The Time . . . Now

As for it taking a lot of time, it's true — it does take time. But its worth the time it takes to teach your child about responsible behavior. Because this father and child were having the same experience every time they got into the car, I suggested that he take a Saturday to teach his child how to behave in the car. Make a big deal out of going to the zoo all week, so the child would know that was where they were going. Then, start out early on Saturday, knowing that it *would* take longer. This trip wouldn't really be about going to the zoo — it would be about teaching responsible behavior.

"What happens if he stops the car, and once the child is getting his attention, the child is quiet, but when he starts the car again, the child begins to scream?" asked another parent.

"Then he should withdraw any positive attention from his child when the car is finally stopped. He could read a book, listen to the radio, hum a tune, and only interact enough to reinforce that when his son stops screaming, they'll continue on their trip to the zoo. It may hurt Dad's ears for a while, but if he's persistent, it should stop the behavior."

By linking the choices that his child made to the consequences that followed those choices, this parent helped his son learn to ride quietly in the car seat. By teaching our children to think through their options, we help them make better choices.

What If My Child *Won't* Choose?

"But what if I tell my child what the choices are, and he says he doesn't choose either one?"

Refusal to choose is a choice in itself. To answer this question, let's think through what happens when, as adults, we choose non-action over action. When we're faced with a choice and we don't act, someone generally chooses for us. Either a boss, or a spouse, or even fate. I suggest that when a child refuses to choose, the parent should say, "If you can't choose, I'll choose for you. And I'll choose _____" (giving the least desirable of the choices offered). Then, ask the child if he would like you to choose. If the child remains silent, or still refuses, then act on the choice you made. Most of the time, children want the control of making the choice themselves, even if neither of the choices is really to their liking. Once they realize that you really will go ahead and choose for them, they'll make their own choice the next time.

Also, a child who refuses to stop his misbehavior, as in the case of the boy screaming in his car seat, is making a choice. By continuing to scream, he is choosing that his father stop the car instead of proceeding to the zoo. This should be stated for him:

"I see you're choosing for me to stop the car. When you've calmed down, then we'll keep going."

Being Creative With Choices

In giving our children choices, it's often the case that the more creative we are, the better. This is especially true when we're having trouble coming up with alternatives, or when we're angry or frustrated and feel we need to resort to punishment.

One mother was having trouble getting her children (ages nine and eleven) to make their beds. She would nag and whine and cajole, but the best she ever got was the bedspread tossed hastily over the rumpled sheets. When she learned about giving choices, she came up with this creative choice for her children: "Either make your beds by 8:30 a.m., or you'll sleep on bare mattresses tonight. Tomorrow morning, I'll give the sheets back to you, and you can try again."

Naturally, her children didn't believe her and left the beds unmade. True to her word, she stripped the beds, and they had to sleep with no covers that night. They didn't make *that* choice again!

Another parent was having trouble getting her eight-year-old son to pick up his clothes. Sometimes the clothes were clean and needed to be hung up, sometimes they were dirty and needed to be put in the clothes hamper. They were *always* all over the house. She came up with this creative choice: "Either pick up your clothes and deal with them appropriately — putting them away if they're clean or in the clothes hamper if they're dirty — or they'll be put in a box in the basement." A week later, her child had no clothes to wear to play with his friends on Saturday. Clean and dirty clothes were mixed in a rumpled heap in a box in the basement, as his mother had promised. After that, he thought twice about leaving his clothes lying around. Though the box stayed and was occasionally put to use, he was much more responsible about his clothes.

Make Your Choices Meaningful

In addition to being creative, it's important that we make the consequences connect to the choices. To tell a child, "Either eat your vegetables or mow the lawn next Saturday," will not teach a child as much as, "Either eat your vegetables or there will be no dessert."

The more closely related the consequence is to the initial problem, the more it simulates the natural consequences that life offers — natural consequences such as climbing a weak tree branch, having it break and falling down, or pulling the cat's tail and having the cat bite you. Natural consequences are the most powerful teachers that exist, and the more we can emulate them, the more our children will learn. As with natural consequences, the consequences you offer your children should not be dangerous in any way. (An excellent guideline for giving choices can be found in the Appendix.)

Choices We Can Live With

When offering choices to our children, it's important that we give choices that we, as parents, can live with. It's also important to structure choices so that siblings don't suffer. For example, if you're at the playground with your two children and one keeps throwing sand at the other children in the sandbox, you wouldn't want to offer the choice, "Either stop throwing sand, or we'll go home." Enforcing that choice makes the sibling who isn't throwing sand suffer. Better to say, "Either stop throwing sand, or get out of the sandbox." That way, you and your other child can stay at the playground, and the only one who experiences the consequence is the one who made the choice.

One parent gave her child a choice she found difficult to live with — yet to her credit, she enforced the choice anyway. She had planned a trip to another city where the family used to live. Her child, five years old at the time, had friends and a nanny there with whom she had been close. Mom had already purchased the plane tickets. A few weeks before the trip, her child had been whining about wanting a particular toy that was popular at the time. The mother gave the choice, "You can either have the toy or the trip to see your friends." Naturally, the child chose the toy, believing, in all probability, that her mother would never cancel the trip and she would get both the toy and the trip.

Her mother returned the tickets. The daughter was intensely disappointed, but her mother did not relent, knowing that if she did, the child would not learn to make responsible choices in the future. Later that week, fate conspired to strengthen the lesson when the toy was lost and never recovered. The mother related that the next time she gave a choice, her daughter said, "I need to think about it, Mommy. I'll tell you my choice soon."

While this is a dramatic story and may seem excessively heavy-handed on the part of the mother, the results speak for themselves. The child began to think her choices through, having learned that choices have consequences that can be difficult to live with.

Choices We *Can't* Live With

What happens, however, when we give our child a choice that we find we *can't* live with? What would have happened, for instance, had the mother in the previous story realized she couldn't return the tickets without an expensive penalty or without disappointing the other people involved? In other words, what happens when we, as parents, speak before *we* think through the consequences of the choices we're offering?

Parents Are Human, Too

Of course, this will happen. We are human, after all, and shouldn't expect to be perfect. The answer is simple — we tell our child we made a mistake. That we gave her a choice that isn't realistic, and we've thought it over and decided on a different choice instead. So in the previous story, had the mother offered the same choice, believing that her child would choose the trip, and found that she could not return the tickets, she could have said, "Wait. You know, I made a mistake. I didn't give you a very realistic choice, because actually, I can't return the plane tickets. We need to start again. You can either wait till your birthday for the toy, or you can buy it with your own money. You choose."

As parents, there's nothing wrong with admitting we didn't think things through. In fact, it may actually serve as a valuable lesson for our children. Being perfect is too demanding a goal for anyone, adult or child. Instead, let's be human and be willing to admit we made a mistake. Then, our children will have role models they can live up to.

Responsibility

Webster's New Collegiate Dictionary defines "responsible" this way: "liable to be called on to answer; able to answer for one's conduct and obligations; able to choose for oneself between right and wrong."

Michael Popkin, in his book *Active Parenting*, says, "Responsibility is a process of making choices and then accepting the consequences of those choices."[6]

Give your children choices and spell out the consequences for them, and you will teach your children to choose for themselves between right and wrong. You won't always be there, looking over their shoulders, when they make the tough choices that life offers. Ensure that they can think through the consequences of their options early in life and help your children be the kind of people who seem to make great choices *all* of the time.

EIGHT

"I Want a Toy!"

Breaking Negative Cycles

The following story may seem dramatized — *if* you've never been in a similar situation as a parent. For those of you who've been through this, it will seem all too familiar. You will know that every word, thought, and feeling is exact, with no exaggeration whatsoever.

An Educational Trip To The Museum

We were at the Planetarium when the gift shop seemed to reach out a hand and entice my daughter inside. (The most exciting area in any museum for children always seems to be the gift shop.) She began with the words, "Buy me something, Mommy," and ran to the books. Though few of them were for children her age (then three-and-a-half), there was one that seemed appropriate, about a magnifying glass. Purchase of the book even included a small magnifying glass with which to experiment, so I encouraged this choice. But my daughter had other ideas, and throwing it back on the shelf, said emphatically,

"I want a *toy!*" After much searching, she found a rubber airplane and a small, fuzzy "critter." She insisted that she wanted them, so I dutifully paid for them. Halfway out the door, however, seeing the books again, she shoved her purchases at me, saying, "I don't want these! I want a book — this book!" (grabbing the one about the magnifying glass).

In any parent's experience, I believe, this type of event "pushes buttons," and I was no different. I immediately "saw red," as my temper flared. I tried to remain calm and told her that she had already made her choice, that we'd already bought her something, and it was time to leave now.

Hysteria ensued. Sobbing. Pleading. Anger. Chaos. Everyone in the shop was staring at me. I could feel their thoughts: "Can't she keep her daughter under control?" I felt panicky.

Taking my daughter by the hand, I said in a low voice, "Emilie, we can't talk about this here. Let's talk in the hallway."

"NO! NO! NO! NO!" Continued hysteria.

"Oh, God," I thought. "What am I doing? I don't know how to deal with this. This is awful."

Shaking, my voice trembling as I attempted to remain in control of myself, I gently pulled her arm as I repeated that we needed to talk in the hallway. "Emilie, the answer to buying the book will be 'no' unless we talk about it in the hallway."

Now that she thought I would give in to buying the book, she came with me (still sobbing and hysterical, though).

What Should I Do?!

We sat down on a bench. I struggled with myself, trying to think of what I would tell another parent to do. Trying to act instead of react. My feelings were all over the place, despair and anger being the most prominent ones. I was amazingly close to tears as I sat on that bench with a hysterical child, trying to get a handle on turning this into a "learning experience" (as my mother used to call it).

There was a long pause. I took a deep breath and decided to try changing some of the negative thoughts I was having into positive ones. As if saying lines to myself (lines I didn't necessarily believe, you understand), I thought, "It's normal for a child to throw tantrums. She's overly tired. I can handle this. I'm a good parent. People are not looking at us, and if they were, it wouldn't matter. This is between my child and myself. We will learn from this. We will grow from this."

The Next Step

Amazingly, I felt calmer. Not a lot, but definitely measurably. Feeling encouraged, I next decided to change what I was doing. I turned to my daughter and summoned up the only empathetic thing I could think of, which wasn't much: "You feel sad about not getting the book."

Although still sobbing, she nodded her head. I felt a bit more in control, but I was still livid. I wasn't sure why. It was confusing. It had been a long time since I'd felt this angry with her.

As my daughter and I sat on the bench together, each struggling with our feelings, it was almost like playing tug of war. I'd acknowledge and accept her feelings, she'd make a plea for the book. I'd say "no," she'd resume hysterics. I was still angry; she was still angry. It was, as they say, a vicious cycle.

After twenty minutes, I decided to see if I could at least take care of *my* feelings. So I asked myself this question: "What do I want her to do differently?" I knew that I couldn't ask her to stop being hysterical, that it wasn't that easy. I decided that I might feel less angry if she apologized, so I simply asked for that. "Emilie, my feelings are hurt, because I already bought you something and you then asked for something else. I think I want you to apologize."

Her tears lessened — sometimes it helps if you just know what another person wants from you. "Mommy, I 'pologize. Can I have the book?"

Try, Try Again

Hmmm. An apology *didn't* make me feel better. I examined my feelings more closely. Why were my feelings hurt? When did they get hurt? Slowly, it became clearer. My feelings got hurt, and I became so angry, when she didn't seem to appreciate what she had — the toys I'd already bought her. Had she really seemed to enjoy them, had she turned to me and said, "I love these, Mommy. Couldn't I please have the book, too?" I would have jumped at the chance to buy her something else. It was the ingratitude that I was having trouble with. I tried again.

"Emmie? Do you know what the word 'appreciate' means?" I asked.

Looking up at me with her tear-streaked face, she nodded, "Yes."

"I guess I'm really angry because you didn't appreciate what I already bought you," I said. "If you had really liked the toys and had told me that you liked them and wanted the book, too, instead of throwing them at me and demanding the book, I probably would have bought the book for you, too. I want you to appreciate the things I give you, or I won't feel like buying anything for you."

Solemnly, and in typical three-year-old fashion, she said, "I 'preciate them. Now can I have the book?"

My voice was sad as I replied, "Those are just words, Em. I don't *know* that you appreciate them."

We sat in silence. Her sobs had subsided. My anger had abated. The minutes ticked by.

"Mommy? Can I have my toys now?"

I gave her the toys.

"Okay," she said. "You be the airplane, and I'll be this one, and I'm coming to your house, okay?"

We began to play. No mention was made of the book. She was, quite simply, enjoying her toys. Fifteen minutes later, it was time to go. We hopped down off the bench, and I turned to her.

"Em? I'd like to buy you that book now if you still want it," I said.

Surprise registered on her face.

"I really feel like you appreciate what I bought you, and that makes me feel like buying you other things, too."

"Okay!" she answered, and we went and bought the book.

Time Well Spent

This incident turned into a valuable lesson for both of us. It was not, however, a lesson that was easily won, nor was it insignificant in the amount of time it took. It's not often that parents feel they have the time to spend forty-five minutes sorting through their feelings and trying different responses. But it must be said that I've seen parents spend the same forty-five minutes arguing with their child. Perhaps the allotment of time remains the same, and the difference is simply in how we fill it.

A Couple Of Pointers

In any case, the point of the preceding dialogue lies in recognizing the cycle we were struggling to break out of. In a moment, we'll discuss negative cycles and what we can do about them. First, let me make two quick points that may have occurred to you as you were reading.

1) While I used the word "appreciate" with my child and she understood it, what would happen if she didn't understand that word? You notice that I asked her first if she understood what it meant. Because she indicated that she did, I continued. Had she shaken her head "no," I would have told her what "appreciate" means.

2) Did I have to buy her the book at the end of this scene? Certainly not. I did so because I felt so good about the exchange we had just had. But what if I couldn't afford the book? Or if I had a second child with me for whom buying the book would create problems? Or if I had run out of time and had to go home? Or if I simply felt the toys were enough? I could just as easily have left the scene after playing with the toys. I might have said something like, "I really enjoyed playing with you. I appreciate that you showed me you liked the toys." I might have even added that next time, maybe we could get the book. Buying the book was *not* a mandatory part of this lesson.

Breaking The Negative Cycle

Now, on to breaking out of negative cycles. It's clear that my daughter and I had engaged in an extremely negative cycle. How did we break out?

Michael Popkin, in his *Family Talk* series, calls these cycles "THINK, FEEL, DO Cycles."[7] Understanding that these cycles occur, and recognizing when they occur, will help us understand how to break out of them. Here's how the THINK, FEEL, DO cycle works:

An **event** occurs. In the previous scenario, the event was my daughter throwing the toys at me and demanding a book instead.

EVENT

toys thrown,
wants book

I felt angry, and panicky, too. I "saw red." Those were my **feelings** about the event. Because our feelings usually follow so quickly after an event occurs, we believe that events cause our feelings:

EVENT

toys thrown,
wants book

FEELINGS

embarrassment, panic,
anger, "saw red"

What we don't realize, however, is that there is a step in between events and feelings, a step that usually occurs so quickly that we don't even realize it happened. That step is our **thoughts** — what we think about the event. It is actually what we think that causes us to feel a certain way. For example:

Suppose you're walking down the street and someone runs past you. How do you feel?

You probably feel neutral, given the lack of information.

But what about this:

You're walking down the street. It's dark and the street is nearly empty of people. Someone runs past you. How do you feel now?

Probably nervous. Why? Because, although the event (someone running past you) remains the same, your thoughts have changed based on the circumstances. This time, your thoughts are probably along the lines of, "Gee, maybe he's running because someone's chasing him." So you may feel nervous, or even a little scared.

Let's try one more:

You're walking down the street. It's 9:00 a.m., and the street is crowded with people going to work. Someone runs past you. How do you feel?

Again, the event has not changed. But your thoughts, based

on the circumstances, are different. Now your thoughts are probably "Gee, I bet he's late to work." As you turn into your workplace, you might feel relieved — good thing you didn't have to run, too!

What Causes What?

The event doesn't cause our feelings. Rather, it is our *thoughts* about the event that cause our feelings.

In the original scenario at the Planetarium, it would look like this:

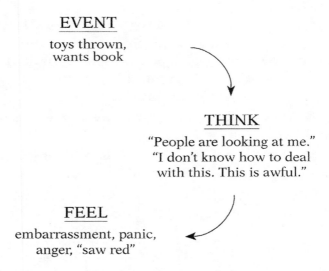

EVENT

toys thrown,
wants book

THINK

"People are looking at me."
"I don't know how to deal
with this. This is awful."

FEEL

embarrassment, panic,
anger, "saw red"

My thoughts of "people are looking at me" caused me to feel embarrassed. Had the museum been empty, this thought would not have occurred, and I wouldn't have felt embarrassed. When I thought, "I don't know how to deal with this. This is awful," I felt panicky.

My feeling of anger, however, wasn't hooked into a thought for me until later, when I became aware that I thought my daughter didn't appreciate what I had already given her. The importance of sorting out our thoughts about an event will become apparent in a moment. Let's complete the cycle first.

When we feel a certain way, we act on our feelings. This is the DO part of the THINK, FEEL, DO cycle. Had I acted on my feelings without trying to break into the cycle in some way, I probably would have punished my daughter. Negative thoughts and feelings produce negative actions. And when you act negatively, the next event will be negative as well:

A COMPLETE NEGATIVE CYCLE

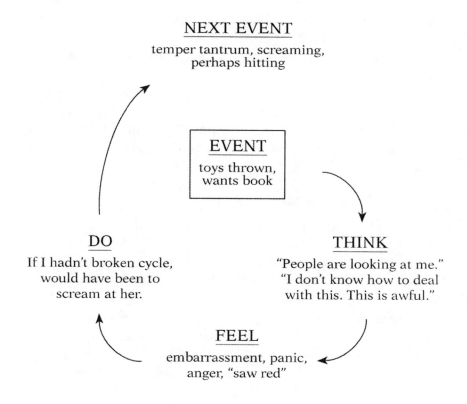

NEXT EVENT
temper tantrum, screaming,
perhaps hitting

EVENT
toys thrown,
wants book

DO
If I hadn't broken cycle,
would have been to
scream at her.

THINK
"People are looking at me."
"I don't know how to deal
with this. This is awful."

FEEL
embarrassment, panic,
anger, "saw red"

Breaking Into The Cycle

When you've recognized a cycle, there are two "windows of opportunity" that give you an opening to break into that cycle and make changes. Those "windows" are what you THINK about the event, and what you DO, sometimes in spite of your feelings.

While at the Planetarium, I made attempts at both windows. I first tried to change my thoughts: "It's normal for a child to throw tantrums. She's overly tired. I can handle this. I'm a good parent. People are not looking at us, and if they were, it wouldn't matter. This is between my child and me. We will learn from this. We will grow from this." These positive thoughts did, indeed, make me feel calmer. Once I felt calmer, I could think more clearly and, therefore, stop myself from doing something negative.

I also tried to break in at the DO window. By taking Emilie's arm and removing her from the immediate situation, I was able to change the next event from a possible tantrum in front of twenty-five people, into sitting on a bench with "simple" hysterics, attracting less attention.

Analyzing My Thoughts And Feelings

But the real breakthrough came later. It may seem as though I acted in a very analytical manner, but it was only through analyzing my anger and attempting to figure out the THOUGHT behind it that I was ultimately able to change an unpleasant event into a learning experience.

I kept wondering, "Why am I angry? What am I thinking that makes me feel so angry?" When I finally realized that I thought she didn't appreciate the toys I'd bought, my feelings changed from anger to sadness, which enabled me to tell her (the DO part of the cycle) what I wanted from her — that she show appreciation. From there, events, thoughts, feelings, and actions went from extremely negative to neutral to positive — she asked for the toys, played with them, and became appreciative.

When you break into a negative cycle by changing your thoughts or action, the next event will be a more positive one:

A COMPLETE POSITIVE CYCLE

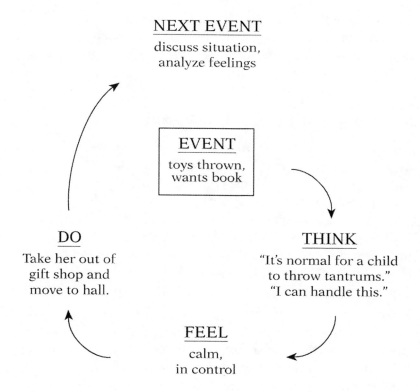

NEXT EVENT
discuss situation,
analyze feelings

EVENT
toys thrown,
wants book

DO
Take her out of
gift shop and
move to hall.

THINK
"It's normal for a child
to throw tantrums."
"I can handle this."

FEEL
calm,
in control

Who "Wins"?

Though at first glance it may seem that my daughter "won" — she did get her book in the end — one mustn't think of these encounters as battles where there is a winner and loser. Rather, they offer an opportunity to strengthen the relationship between parent and child, and a means for parents to teach their children some very important lessons about values, feelings, and expectations.

My child learned something valuable at the Planetarium, and it wasn't about the stars: she learned how to act when she receives a gift, and how the giver feels when a gift isn't appreciated. She learned something about manners that a simple, "Say thank you, Emilie," could never have taught. And she also learned something about the values in the family in which she is growing up — a lesson that will last a lifetime.

An Important Lesson For Parents

I learned something valuable, too. I learned that controlling our children is not the ultimate goal, but that *teaching* them is. And teaching our children requires that we understand a lot about ourselves first — why we feel the way we do, why we think the way we do. It is only in understanding our THINK, FEEL, DO cycle that we can understand ourselves, and only in understanding ourselves that we can change the events in both our children's lives and our own.

I also learned an important lesson about patience. Patience doesn't necessarily mean remaining calm, cool, and collected, but it does mean investing some time — because it takes a lot of time to teach the lessons our children need to learn. And the investment of time is one of the most worthwhile investments you'll ever make!

Take The Time

The next time a battle begins with your child, remember the THINK, FEEL, DO cycle. Remember that your windows of opportunity to break the cycle are your **thoughts** and your **actions**. Why do you feel the way you do? What are your thoughts? Can you change your thoughts?

Once you know what you feel and why you feel that way, what

do you want the next event to be? What would you have to do differently to make that next event happen the way you want it to? Can you think of something you can ask your child to do differently? Can you think of something *you* can do differently?

Think to yourself: What is my child learning by the way I'm handling this situation? Is he learning a valuable lesson, or is he merely learning that I'm in control? What can I think or do that will make this lesson more valuable?

Finally, the next time a battle begins, take the *time*. It's an investment you won't regret — in your child's future, in your own future, in your family's future, and in the future of your relationship with your child.

NINE

NO MEANS NO

DIMINISHING YOUR CHILD'S
USE OF THE WORD "NO"

Perhaps one of the most frustrating experiences for parents of a toddler is when the answer to everything the parent says or asks is "NO!" This is one of the more exasperating characteristics of the period commonly called the "terrible twos."

While as parents, we would not want to eliminate the word "no" from our child's vocabulary (in fact, it's valuable when used appropriately), we do want to diminish its frequency and encourage appropriate usage.

There are two basic ways in which parents can diminish their child's inappropriate use of the word "no." You can begin both of these as early as you wish — preferably as the child is beginning to be verbal, when he has only one or two words in his speaking vocabulary.

TECHNIQUE #1

Teach your child the meaning of "yes" and "no."

When Betty and Don's child, William, was about eighteen months old, he was sitting on the rug in their living room fussing. Because of the time of day and because she knew his routine, Betty was pretty sure that he was thirsty and got him a bottle of apple juice. As she approached him, with the bottle extended, she said "Will, do you want some apple juice?"

"No!" was the reply.

Betty immediately withdrew the bottle. "Okay," she said, turning around and heading back to the kitchen. William looked surprised, then burst into tears.

Betty turned back. "William? It sounds as though you *do* want the bottle after all, but you have to say 'yes' when I ask you instead of 'no.' Otherwise I'll take it away. Do you want the bottle?"

William, his tears still fresh on his cheeks, looked at her.

"You have to say 'yes,' Will, if you want the bottle. Do you want the bottle?" Betty repeated.

"'Es?" William tentatively offered.

"Okay," said Betty. William took the bottle gratefully.

Sound easy? Sure. But many parents don't do this, believing that they know what their child wants better than their child does. In the example above, Betty did indeed know that William wanted juice, but instead of ignoring his "no" and perhaps placing the bottle beside him, she took the opportunity to teach William that words have meanings and those meanings have consequences.

It's important to note that this wasn't the last time that William said "no" when he meant "yes." Children learn through repetition, and Betty had to repeat this lesson with toys, food, books. But by taking William at his word when he said "no," she effectively diminished it's *inappropriate* use. Instead of William using "no" as a power word, he began to think carefully about whether "no" was appropriate for his needs before he used it. The result was a "terrible two-year-old" who more often said "yes!" than "no!"

A Hint

Don't ask your child "yes" and "no" questions when they don't really have a choice about it. For example, if Betty had an appointment for which she was late and she asked William, "Are you ready yet?", she would have had to ignore his "no" and get him ready anyway. A better question in this instance would be, "Do you want to put your coat on inside the apartment, or when we get out into the hallway?" A reply of "no" to this question can then be answered with, "That's not part of the choice — either inside or in the hallway, William." Further "no's" would then result in Mom responding with, "If you can't choose, I'll choose for you, and I'll choose that you put it on in here."

The trick here is to think ahead before you ask your child a "yes" or "no" question, so that you can be ready to take him at his word.

Another Hint

Don't be fooled by a child who is not completely verbal yet. Quite a few parents believe that because their child can't verbalize her thoughts, she must not understand the question. This leads to parents ignoring when their child says "no" as well. Assume that your child *does* understand your questions, even if she doesn't. Children learn from actions, and taking the bottle away in response to a "no" answer will make the meaning of your original question clear, even if it wasn't clear to begin with. If you are gentle in your tone of voice, demeanor and facial expression, your child will understand that this is just a normal interaction and not a punishment. Always remember that you are your child's teacher, and the lesson here is about word meanings.

TECHNIQUE #2

Use the word yourself *only* in emergencies.

As children grow and become more mobile, it becomes necessary for parents to place limits on their behavior. These limits ensure the child's safety (i.e., stopping him from touching a hot radiator), as well as ensuring the safety of your property (i.e., stopping him from playing with your crystal flower vase).

Most parents use the word "no" to place limits on their children. Because this occurs so often with a newly mobile child, the child may hear the word "no" fifty to one hundred times a day or more.

When a word is heard that often, it loses its power, and children become apathetic to it.

For example, when a parent says, "No, honey, don't pick that up off the floor," "Sweetie, Mommy said 'no,' don't climb on the back of the couch," "No, William, don't go in the kitchen," "No, don't pull the dog's tail, that's a no-no," and follows it all with, "No! Don't touch the radiator!", it makes the "no" in front of "don't touch the radiator" pretty meaningless. In other words, it's lost its power.

In addition, when the word "no" is used frequently, children are apt to use it themselves, because they've heard it so often. Child educators have long known that repetition is one way in which children learn. Remembering that we are our children's teachers, if *we* use the word "no" repeatedly, we must realize that we are helping our *child* learn to use the word repeatedly.

What Else Can I Do?

So what's the solution? It's obvious that we need to use the word sparingly, so that it won't lose its power when we need it most — in emergencies — and so that our children don't hear it so often that they think its *supposed* to precede every sentence.

The solution is to use the word "no" *only* in emergencies, i.e., when your child is about to touch a hot stove or run in front of an oncoming car.

However, by telling you to use the word "no" only in emergencies, I am *not* telling you to be a permissive parent and let your child get away with murder. You still need to set limits on your child for his safety and yours. What's needed is a substitute for the word "no" which has the same effect.

Using A Substitute

Here is the substitute:

Description + Choice

By first describing to the child the function of an object, then giving him a choice about what he *can* do (instead of just what he *can't* do), you can create limits within which your child feels he has some freedom (he'll rebel less), and that still preserve his (and your home's) safety. In addition, by keeping the choices to what he *can* do, the child will learn to look for positive alternatives to his behavior, instead of just negative outcomes.

How It's Done — The Preverbal Child

Robert's baby, Charlotte, who had just begun to crawl and was still putting things in her mouth, found a small piece of paper on the floor. Cooing excitedly, she immediately picked it up and began to put it in her mouth. Robert walked to her quickly, gently put his hand over hers (and over the paper), and said:

"Charlotte, paper is not for putting in your mouth." (Description)

He reached for a nearby toy that was safe for her to chew on, as he gently removed the paper from her hand, saying "You can either put this in your mouth," handing her the toy, "or you may put this in your mouth." Glancing quickly around the room, he spotted a teething ring and handed it to her, thus giving her a choice of two positive alternatives. (Choice)

By using Description + Choice, Robert effectively stated a limit (no paper in mouth) without using the word "no."

Had the paper been a toxic cleansing agent, however, Robert would have wanted to use the word "NO!" immediately, emphatically, and without hesitation — toxic cleansing agents present a dangerous situation.

By combining Action with Description + Choice (Dad moved to Charlotte, put his hand over hers, and gently removed the paper as he spoke), instead of simply talking to her from across the room, he also ensured that she understood what his meaning was, even though she was preverbal. Once children become verbal, they will respond to the Description + Choice without necessarily requiring action on the part of the parent, but preverbal children need the combination.

How It's Done — The Verbal Child

Now let's talk about the verbal child — one who doesn't require the combination of Action with Description + Choice. Perhaps the child is too old to take something away from him without a physical struggle. For this child, the action takes place primarily *after* the Description + Choice, not during, as it does with the preverbal child.

Mary's five-year old, Brad, had been peacefully playing with Play-Doh on the floor. The cat strolled by, and Brad decided the Play-Doh could easily be transformed into a hand grenade. Yelling, "Look out! It's the enemy!", he launched his Play-Doh grenade into the air, fortunately missing the cat, but hitting the opposite wall, where it made a red smudge.

Mary, staying calm, said, "Brad, Play-Doh is not for throwing; it's for making shapes with." (Description) "You may either make shapes with it without throwing it, or put it away." (Choice)

Brad, thoroughly entranced with his game now, either didn't hear his mother or chose to ignore her. In any case, while she was talking, he wadded up another ball of Play-Doh and, spotting the cat, launched another grenade. This time, it hit its mark, and the cat yowled and leaped, hissing, into the air.

Mary calmly walked over to the Play-Doh, scooped it up and said, "I see you've chosen to put the Play-Doh away."

Brad's eyes widened, and he stammered, "But, but Mom! I didn't know. I don't want to put it away, please?"

Mary remained firm as she continued to gather the Play-Doh. "I'm sorry you didn't hear me, Brad, but Play-Doh is not for throwing, and you even hurt the cat. I gave you a choice to either make shapes with it without throwing it, or to put it away. I know it's hard to live with some choices, like putting it away, but you'll have a chance to try again later."

(The chance to try again later helps the child to develop responsibility and to remember how he needs to behave with the object in question. For young children, the chance to try again should occur pretty quickly, perhaps even within an hour or so. For older children, like Brad, the chance to try again can occur the next day.)

You might be wondering if Mary should have repeated herself, since she wasn't sure if Brad had actually heard the choice she gave him. The answer is no. If Mary assumes he hasn't heard her and repeats herself, Brad learns that there is an advantage to not listening, and he gets paid off in the end. His payoff is either in gaining time, making his mother angry or frustrated, or getting a second chance right away.

A Second Chance

But why shouldn't Mary go ahead and give Brad a second chance right away? Especially if Brad seems contrite and genuinely sorry — he may even pledge that if he gets a second chance right away, he won't ever throw Play-Doh again.

This is a tough one on most parents. It's difficult to see our children in distress — even if it's caused by a choice they have made. And it's doubtful that any parent can remain firm in enforcing their child's choices all the time.

But remember that there are two important questions to ask yourself when you're tempted to make peace and give your child a second chance right away, and these two things hold true for *all* of our dealings with our children. Whether you are setting limits or making decisions about whether to enforce choices, *always* ask yourself these two questions:

1) Is what I'm doing working?

2) What am I teaching my child by doing this?

In the case of Brad and giving him a second chance right away, the answer to "Is what I'm doing working?" is "It may work, but the lesson is definitely weakened by allowing him to take back his choice."

The answer to the second question, "What am I teaching my child by doing this?" is "I'm teaching him that he doesn't need to listen when I speak, that a *show* of contriteness will weaken my stand on an issue, and that he probably can misbehave in other ways, because I give second chances."

Again, for a parent to remain firm all the time is next to impossible, but ultimately, remaining firm *most* of the time will be far more beneficial to both you and your child.

One final note about choices and remaining firm: it's important to remember that while it may seem inconsequential to *you* to allow second chances on the choices a young child makes, when the child gets older, he'll be faced with choices for which there are no second chances. Choices about sex, alcohol, and other drugs, among others. Being firm now will save both of you a lot of grief in the long run. And don't forget — for small children, what we see as small choices may seem monumental to them. When you allow them to take back *any* choice, they feel as though they've won a major victory.

One More Hint

To conclude, let me give you one final reminder about the choices you'll be giving.

Don't give your child choices that are unacceptable to you. For example, don't say, "You may play properly with the Play-Doh, or I'll throw it away," if throwing it away isn't something you're willing to carry out. Otherwise, you'll be stuck in a situation where you *can't* remain firm, your child will recognize which choices you're unlikely to carry through on, and he'll take advantage of that opportunity by continuing to misbehave.

Remember, being firm now will make it easier — for both of you — when your child's choices become more crucial or life-threatening.

TEN

A MAGICIAN IN THE LIVING ROOM

GETTING RID OF BEDTIME BLUES

One of the most common questions I am asked is about sleep routines. "How can we have a bedtime without a fight?" "Bedtime takes an hour and a half, and we still fight. Is there any way around this?"

The answer is a qualified "yes." Qualified because it takes patience and persistence, and because it depends on the age of your child.

To understand the solution, one must first understand how children feel about going to bed. To do that, I'd like you to imagine this:

Your Child's Point Of View

You're sitting in your living room, gathered with the people you love and admire most. In the room is also a magician. He's doing the most incredible magic you've ever seen. Not only that, but he's letting you examine the tricks as he goes along, and it appears that there is no trick — it's really magic! Balls disappear into thin air, paper is torn in pieces, only to reappear whole. You're dazzled and amazed and having a wonderful time.

Suddenly, a giant appears, three or four times taller than you. An arm swoops down, and you're lifted into the air. You're taken by the giant into the bathroom, where he demands that you brush your teeth and go to the bathroom. All the time, you hear the "oohs" and "ahhs" of the people in your living room. There is even the sound of applause. You *know* you're missing the best tricks of all.

The giant then picks you up again, carries you to your room and demands that you fall asleep. The door closes behind him, and you can still hear the laughter, applause, and sounds of amazement coming from the room you are no longer in.

Would you be willing to go to sleep?

Obviously, there aren't circus acts going on in your living room as you try to put your child to bed. You may even be very quiet during your child's bedtime routine. But resistance occurs because as children grow, they develop a sense of the world as being separate from themselves. Before this, your child had thought of the world as revolving around her — when she opened her eyes, the world, with all its activities and interests, began; when she shut her eyes, the world ceased to exist. But now, her mind has taken an important leap ahead. She has a sense that she may be missing something once she falls asleep, and she's very reluctant to have that happen. While whatever is going on may not be as interesting and exciting as a magician, it's still more interesting than going to sleep.

How Can We Help?

Many times, parents approach the child who is resistant to bedtime with an attitude of, "How can we make this easier for *us* (the parents)?" But we're more likely to find the answer if we understand how difficult it is for our *child* and instead ask the question, "How can we make this easier for our child?"

The answer is somewhat involved, but certainly not difficult to implement. It has two basic components:

1) Preparation

2) Ritualization

And it requires two attitudes:

1) Firmness

2) Confidence

PREPARATION

Let's look at the first component of making bedtime easier, that of **preparation**. The need for preparation comes from the realization that bedtime is a transition, and while some children handle transitions more easily than others, *all* children need guidance of some sort through the transitions that take place on a daily basis in their lives.

Transitions occur many times throughout each day — when you're leaving the house to take your child to the playground, dropping him off at school, getting him into the bathtub, having company come over for dinner. A little preparation will go a long way to ease your child through these transition times.

Handling Transitions

Begin by giving your child warning that a transition (in this case bedtime) is approaching.

Half an hour before bedtime, say to your child, "In half an hour, it will be time to start the routine." (Routine is a good word to use, because it's a summary of the entire process you'll be implementing, and ultimately you'll be able to say to a resistant child, "Do you want to do the routine, or skip it and go straight to bed?")

Give another warning at fifteen minutes and again at five minutes. When it's time to begin the routine, say, "Now it's time to start the routine and go to bed."

Warnings help a child to make sense out of what seems, much of the time, to be a very chaotic and arbitrary existence. They give the child a sense of order, avoid unpleasant surprises, and give him a feeling of control — things aren't being done *to* him, but *with* him.

How Your Child May React

Your child may have a variety of reactions to this warning system.

1) He may feel calm and confident and go quietly to bed after months of having fought with you. If this happens, thank your lucky stars and celebrate!

2) He may begin resistance at the half hour call, saying (or screaming), "No bed! No bed!" or something along those lines. Here is where the two components of your attitude will come into play — be firm and confident. Say, "Not now, in thirty (or fifteen or five) minutes."

3) He may wait patiently through the warnings, but when it's time to actually initiate the routine, begin screaming and resisting. If this happens, be firm and confident, and say, "Well, you have a choice. You can either do the routine, or you can skip it and go straight to bed. What would you like to do?" Most of the time, the child will choose the routine — after all, it does allow them to stay up that much later. "Straight-to-bed" doesn't usually sound like an acceptable alternative to a child.

Testing

Be prepared, however, for your child to test and see if you really mean that they can choose straight-to-bed and that you will enforce it. Children test, because, as parents, we tend to waver about our decisions in order to keep the peace. In the past, you might have given in and allowed five more minutes. Or you may have allowed your child to change his choice, letting him "take back" what he said because he seemed genuinely contrite, or he said he's "changed his mind" when it becomes clear you're going to follow through on the choice he made. The following story illustrates this:

Routine Or No Routine

Until the time their child was three, Sally and Richard had no difficulty with Michelle's bedtime routine. They had been consistent, giving her warnings to ease the transition and generally following the same routine for well over a year. All three seemed comfortable, and things ran smoothly. Then, disaster struck!

Two family friends whose company Michelle deeply enjoyed had come over for dinner. After dinner, Sally told Michelle, "In ten minutes, it'll be time to start the routine." Michelle seemed to accept this. Sally also gave the five minute warning without any protest. But when Sally said, "Michelle, now it's time to begin the routine," Michelle began to whine, "I don't want to go to bed. I don't want to brush my teeth. Please, can I stay up?"

Richard chimed in, "Michelle, you have a choice. You can either begin the routine now without whining, or skip it and go straight to bed. What would you like to do?" Michelle said, "But I don't want to. I want to stay up. Please? Just five more minutes."

"Michelle," said Richard, "if you delay any longer, then I'll assume you're choosing to skip the routine. Either go get your toothbrush right now, or skip the routine. You decide." Michelle, in the dramatic and, at times, endearing way that three-year-olds have, flopped on the couch with her arms spread wide, exhaled loudly and switched tactics: "I'm too *tired* to brush my teeth."

To his credit, Richard did not let the switch of technique bother him. In a firm, calm voice, he said, "Okay, Michelle, I can see you'd rather skip the routine tonight. Let's get you to bed." And with that, he scooped her up and began to carry her out of the room.

As you can imagine, Michelle became hysterical. Once she realized that Richard meant what he said, she turned to her mother. "Mommy, Mommy!" The sobs were heartrending. "Help me!" Sally, who had to take a deep breath first (here's the confidence aspect of the technique), said quietly, "Honey, I agree with your Daddy. You chose to skip the routine. You'll have a chance to try again tomorrow."

"Please, please, PLEASE! Just listen!" sobbed Michelle, as Richard began to take her out of the room. Respectfully, Richard stopped. "I'm sorry," sobbed Michelle. "Really. I will *never* do it again. Please let me have the routine. I'm sorry! Please!"

Richard gave her a hug and sympathized, "Honey, I'm sorry you feel bad about your choice. Sometimes it's hard to live with our choices. But you'll have a chance to try again tomorrow." And with that, he carried her to bed, still crying.

The Underlying Lesson

It took a great deal of courage on the part of Sally and Richard not to allow Michelle to take back her choice. After all, Michelle sounded contrite, almost desperately so. She seemed truly sorry she'd chosen to skip the routine. Even her change of heart appeared genuine. In essence, she seemed to be saying, "I've thought it over. I've learned my lesson."

But had Sally and Richard allowed her to change her mind at that point, the lesson she would have learned would have been very different from the one she was claiming to have learned.

Instead of learning that her choices have consequences, she would have learned that *enough tears and a display of contriteness (genuine or not) can change the outcome of the choices she makes.*

Serious Consequences . . .

While this example may seem trivial, the lesson it teaches is not. If your teenager chooses to have unprotected sex and gets pregnant or contracts AIDS, no one — not you, not your child — *no one* can take that choice back. As parents, we must not wait for our children to experience consequences that are disastrous in order for them to learn about the consequences they will face as adults.

. . . Or Positive Outcomes

It is only through structuring your child's environment and allowing him to experience *unpleasant* but *safe* consequences, without taking them back, that you can be assured that your child will continue to develop the ability to think through his choices before he makes them. This skill will not only enable your child to survive in today's society by making the right choices in dangerous situations, but will also prevent him from feeling victimized by circumstances. He'll learn to take responsibility for the choices he makes — provided, of course, that his parents don't rush in to "fix it" and take those choices back from him, just because the consequences may be unpleasant.

RITUALIZATION

The second part of having a calm bedtime is **ritualization**. Rituals accompany many of the large transitions that occur during a person's lifetime. Taking a partner for life is accompanied by a wedding ceremony, for example. Likewise, death is accompanied by a funeral or memorial service, baby showers are given as part of the ritual for having a child, and so on.

Many of the "smaller" transitions we face, however, are not marked by a ritual — losing a job, changing homes, moving to another part of the country. These transitions tend to be filled with stress and anxiety — tensions that have not been eased by the accompaniment of a ritual.

For your child, bedtime is a significant transition, and like all transitions, can be eased by implementing a ritual.

The Bedtime Ritual

The bedtime ritual will be unique for your family. It should be based on the things you and your child enjoy, like reading or storytelling, and include the things necessary in getting ready for bed, such as brushing teeth and going to the bathroom.

A few factors should be considered when designing the ritual for your child:

1) Always begin the ritual with the preparation, as described earlier in this chapter (time warnings).

2) Include the "work" part of getting ready for bed within the ritual framework. In other words, taking a bath, brushing teeth, combing hair, getting pajamas on, going to the bathroom — anything your child is required to do in the evening before bed.

3) Adopt a "work first, play later" philosophy. All the drudgery of bedtime (brushing teeth, getting pajamas on) should come first, and the enjoyable parts (reading a story, nighttime kisses, a backrub) should come last. This way, if your child refuses to carry out one of the requirements, you can give him a choice to skip the whole routine and go straight to bed. That means your child will have to consider skipping *all* of what he enjoys just to get out of *one* of the things he doesn't

enjoy. Keep in mind that if your child skips the necessities, such as brushing teeth or going to the bathroom, there will be no long-term negative effects, even if he should wet the bed — he will learn from that as well. In my experience, it's highly unlikely that your child will skip the routine more than once.

4) Keep the ritual fairly simple, with clear steps that don't vary, so your child will know what to expect.

5) When you get to the final step of your ritual, don't let your child talk you into repeating a step. Be firm that the end of the ritual has come, and you're going to see him in the morning. Then leave the room with firmness, confidence, and grace.

An Example

To give you a clear example of what a bedtime ritual is, let's look at a ritual that David used after his divorce, whenever his five-year-old daughter, Sarah, was visiting. (Note: It's especially important that rituals be observed in situations where divorce is involved and the child is visiting the non-custodial parent. Because the situation itself may cause feelings of insecurity, it is crucial that the transitions the child experiences in their "home away from home" are ritualized. This will help the child feel that there's a sense of order in the arrangement, which will ultimately make her feel more secure and more in control.)

Remember that this is just an example. Your ritual may look very different from this one — rituals should be based on an individual family's values.

DAVID'S BEDTIME RITUAL FOR SARAH

1) Prepare Sarah by giving fifteen, ten, and five minute warnings. Then tell her that it's time to begin the routine.

2)   Things Sarah must do before story time:
   a) Brush teeth
   b) Go potty
   c) Put on nightie
   d) Put toys away
   e) Climb into bed
3)   Give Sarah a choice of which book to read — Dad chooses two, she can choose one of the two for him to read.
4)   Sit on edge of bed and read story.
5)   Give Sarah a drink of water and play a game (checkers, Old Maid, Go Fish).
6)   Put cup of water on nightstand.
7)   Plug in night light.
8)   Close closet door.
9)   Say, "I love you, Sarah. I'll see you first thing in the morning."
10) Dad leaves the room, closing door behind him.

Even The Same Words?

While it may seem stilted or stiff to go so far as to ritualize the words we use to say "good night," think about the rituals for adult transitions — there are ritualized words for weddings, funerals, graduation.

Keeping the words almost the same each night gives the child a sense of security about the transition of sleep. There is security in knowing that if you said last night that you would see her first thing in the morning and you did, then the same thing will happen tomorrow morning as well.

Some Common Mistakes

Preparation and ritualization will go a long way towards making bedtime a positive experience for both you and your child. As you begin to analyze, change, or introduce these elements into your early evening hours, let me prepare you further by helping you avoid some common mistakes parents make.

ACTIVE PLAY

Many times, parents will try to involve their child in very active play right before the bedtime ritual. They do this believing that it will tire their child out and the child will go to bed more willingly. Unfortunately, active play often has the opposite result — it has a tendency to overstimulate. Overstimulation adds to the "magician in the living room" effect — not only is the child having a great time and is unwilling to stop, he is also all wound up because of the activity. A child who has been overstimulated will find it almost impossible to approach bedtime with anything less than extreme resistance.

TELEVISION

Another common mistake parents make involves television. While many children can watch TV in the evening without becoming overstimulated, it's important to keep in mind that TV, while a passive medium, can be stimulating and possibly even addictive.

One of my clients came to me because her daughter (age seven) was getting up in the middle of the night, saying she had nightmares, and that it was "safer" in Mommy's bed. After some discussion, it became evident that TV was included as part of the bedtime ritual, and that often her daughter would fall asleep watching television, to be carried to bed by Mom later. While it may seem to you, as it did to this mother, that the TV was effectively making her child drowsy, the sleep that followed was not a restful one. TV had actually overstimulated her daughter, causing vivid (and sometimes nightmarish) dreams.

Your child may not seem as drowsy and "prepared" for sleep after reading a book as she does after watching TV, but book reading and gentle talking are far more effective ways to engage your child in restful instead of stimulated sleep.

If your child is still wide awake after you've read to her, remember that there's nothing wrong with allowing her to read or look quietly at her books after you've left the room. She may need that "alone time" as part of her own private ritual.

LYING DOWN WITH THE CHILD

Many parents lie down with their child until the child dozes off. Depending upon what you want out of your evening, this may or may not present difficulties. Many of the parents I counsel and teach begin this routine to help their child fall asleep faster, so that they can have more time to themselves in the evening. While this may work for awhile, most parents find that once the child gets used to it, one of three things happens: (1) the child takes *longer* to fall asleep, because he is enjoying the parent's company in bed; (2) the child dozes off, only to awaken each time the parent makes an attempt to leave; or (3) the parent becomes one of the child's "sleep associations," like the teddy bear, pillow or night light, that he needs to *stay* asleep.

Thus, parents who do this so that they can have *more* time for themselves in the evening often find themselves robbed of that time. If you view the evening hours after your child has gone to bed as precious, it's better not to lie down with your child as part of his routine.

If you've already instituted this as part of the routine, but have found that it backfired, stop now. Do this by saying to your child, "I realize I've been treating you like a baby by sleeping next to you. You're a big boy/girl now, and I know you can fall asleep by yourself. We'll do all the other parts of the routine, but I'm not going to lie down in bed with you anymore." Follow this up by not giving in. And be prepared for crying and screaming. It's unlikely that your child will willingly give this up. Stay strong by keeping in mind what you want in the evening, and by realizing that it is valuable for your child to find ways to comfort himself and to learn how to fall asleep by himself.

Getting Out Of Bed

A discussion of bedtime wouldn't be complete without mention of what to do when your child either gets out of bed once she's been kissed goodnight or calls out for you after bedtime. Sometimes this occurs in the middle of the night, sometimes right after the end of the routine. Unfortunately, it can also occur many times throughout the evening, disturbing either your much needed "alone time" or your own sleep.

There are three basic reasons why a child gets out of bed: (1) she is seeking attention and trying to delay bedtime; (2) she is fearful; or (3) she is having trouble satisfying her own needs and wants Mommy or Daddy to satisfy them for her. Let's cover these one at a time.

DELAYING BEDTIME

The first, and most obvious, is to delay bedtime further. A child will either plead for another drink of water, say that she has to go to the bathroom, or come out to tell you something she's forgotten about. The child who repeatedly gets up to delay bedtime is often seeking the attention of her parents as well. Because some of the excuses seem valid to parents (i.e., going to the bathroom), they are likely to allow this behavior. Moreover, they pay attention to the child when she comes out of her room, many times even going back in the room to tuck the child in. This attention compounds the problem, because attention is a large part of what the child is seeking in the first place.

There are several steps parents can take to combat this bedtime challenge.

1) Make sure that all of your child's needs are taken care of in the routine: she's gone to the bathroom, there is a drink of water accessible to her in her bedroom, and that you've asked if she has anything more to tell you *before* you leave the room. If your child comes up with an excuse for getting out of bed that I haven't listed, incorporate it into the routine as well.

2) Give a minimum of attention to a child who gets up. If she insists that she has to go to the bathroom, allow her to — by herself. (Make sure that the bathroom light is left on for those children too small to reach the switch, otherwise that will be added to the list of excuses.) Use encouraging words like "Okay, that's something you can do for yourself." Try not to take your attention away from what you were doing before your child got out of bed. Focusing your attention on your child will encourage her to continue this behavior.

   If your child asks to be tucked in again, use your discretion, but be aware that if this particular bedtime challenge has been ongoing, and if she gets out of bed several times throughout the evening, it's best not to tuck her in again. Better to say, "We already did the routine, and I tucked you in once. When you get out of bed, you have to be responsible for tucking yourself back in." Be polite, but firm on this point, or your child will get in and out of bed in order to get the attention that being tucked in provides.

3) Finally, if the problem continues, you will need to find what I call a "key" that will guide you in finding a consequence for your child getting out of bed. When I counsel parents, I ask them to tell me exactly what their child *needs* in order to sleep. Maybe your child sleeps with the bedroom door open, maybe she uses a night light, maybe she has to have all the stuffed animals in bed with her. These are what I call "keys" that you can use if the first two steps don't work.

Finding The "Key"

Let's see how Randy and Sharon used their child's "key" to help him stay in bed.

When Sharon called me, she sounded desperate. Her son, Toby (two years old), would get up ten times after having been tucked into bed. Each time, either Sharon or Randy would escort him back to his bed. After closing the door, however, they could still hear him playing with his toys and knew it was only a matter of time before he came out again. Sharon said this had been going on for some time, so that now every creak of the floorboards or sound of footsteps made her tense in anticipation of the forthcoming battle. When they called me, their evenings had become extremely stressful, and they spent even the few minutes they had together listening to see if Toby was getting out of bed.

After we talked for some time, I saw that they had already instituted some routine in Toby's bedtime, and they were attempting to give him a minimum of attention when he arose. But neither of those had worked. It was time for Step Three — figuring out a key that could be used as a consequence for Toby if he got out of bed.

Sharon and Randy said there were two requirements that had to be fulfilled for Toby to sleep: he wanted a lamp on that threw a dim light over the room, and he always asked for more than one stuffed animal to sleep with. They also told me that the door to his room was shut when he slept. I chose the lamp to be the key that they would work with.

I told them that the first step would be to put Toby to bed as usual, but that the first time he got out of bed, one of them should give him an "I" message: "When you get up out of bed, I feel frustrated, because it takes away from Mommy and Daddy's alone time. I would like you to stay in bed once we've done the routine."

I warned them that he would probably go back to bed, but get up again. The importance of giving the "I" message first, I stressed, was that by linking it with the action that would follow, Toby would eventually respond to the "I" message alone. So, when he got out of bed the second time, I told them they should tell him that they were concerned that the light was keeping him awake, and that he could either go back to his room and go to sleep, or they would turn the light off to help him sleep better.

If he got up a third time, one of them should say, "I can see the light is keeping you awake. Let's turn it off so that you can get to sleep." Then I advised them to turn off the light, but because in their particular circumstances it would cast his room into pitch darkness, either Mom or Dad should stay in the room just inside the door.

When Toby cried, whoever was in his room should then say, "Sounds like you aren't happy with the choice you made. But Toby, when you get up, I think the light is keeping you awake. If you can stay in bed and go to sleep with the light on, that would be okay, but when you get up, you choose to turn the light off so you can sleep better."

Then, I told them to offer him a chance to try again right away, saying, "Would you like to try again?" Undoubtedly, he would say "yes," and it was my guess that he wouldn't test and get up again that night. In the upcoming evenings, I suggested that they remind him during the routine that he could choose to have the light on and go right to sleep, or he could get up, but then choose to have the light off. Then, they should be prepared to carry through immediately by turning the light off if he got up.

I also told them that, while some parents had immediate success, this method might take some time, and they should be patient and persistent. I asked them to call me the next week to follow up.

THE RESULT

When the day of the follow-up arrived, I waited with great anticipation to hear what results they'd achieved. Sharon got on the phone first, and she was breathless with excitement. "It worked! In fact, it worked so well, I can't believe it!" Then Randy broke in. "It worked the first night, and we haven't had a problem since then. Even the babysitter did it, and he's gone right to bed each time." Sharon's voice overlapped Randy's. "I just can't believe that it's finally over." She chuckled a little. "I still jump at the floorboards creaking, but not as much as I used to."

"Did he test you at all?" I asked.

Randy replied, "Actually, no. We gave him the 'I' message, and then we told him that we were concerned that the light was keeping him awake, and told him we would turn it off if it would help him sleep, but we never had to turn it off. He went right to bed after that, and every night afterward as well. Thank you so much!"

I smiled. "You're the ones who did the work. All you needed was an idea and the courage to remain firm. You did great — you should be proud of yourselves!"

Sharon and Randy did achieve a great success. By using a key, they were able to provide a consequence for Toby that would encourage him to stay in bed.

Finding Your Own Key

To get you thinking about what key you can use in your own particular circumstances, here are two other common keys, with suggestions on how to include them into a format similar to the one Sharon and Randy used:

1) If your child prefers to sleep with the door to his room open, tell him that you're afraid the noise is keeping him awake, and it will be quieter if you shut the door.

2) If your child must sleep with loads of stuffed animals, tell him you think that he's too crowded in bed, and that must be why he's getting up. Tell him that you'll put the animals on his shelf, so that he can sleep more easily.

These, as well as the night light, are the three main keys that are appropriate in most parents' cases. If none of these is appropriate for you — in other words, if your child sleeps without toys or other sleep associations, with the light off and the door shut, but still gets out of bed several times during the evening — you might look for keys that immediately precede bedtime. For example, maybe he wrestles with his Dad. This can be a key as well, and you can tell him that perhaps wrestling is overstimulating, and he should skip it the next night.

Obviously, it's better to find a key that occurs during your child's sleep patterns, and not before. Otherwise you'll have to wait until the next evening to enforce the consequence. In either case, if you think long enough, you're sure to find your own key — something that your child finds important to his comfort in sleeping or in his bedtime routine — that you can use to encourage him to stay in bed.

FEARFULNESS

The second main reason that a child will either get out of bed or call out for his parents is that he is fearful. By about age fourteen months, children sometimes develop a fear of the dark. According to Frank and Theresa Caplan, in their book, *The Second Twelve Months of Life*, this fear develops because the toddler becomes capable of playing out roles and enacting fantasies — in other words, he begins playing imaginatively. With this developmental leap comes the ability to "play out scary characters in dreams and in nightmares. . . Nightmares are an outgrowth of a child's ability to think on a symbolic level." They further suggest that it is not until about the age of four years that the child will be able to distinguish between reality and fantasy.[8]

The ability to think on a symbolic level is a huge step for children. It's an important part of becoming someone who will function well in the adult world and should be recognized and celebrated as such. But this doesn't solve the practical problem of getting your child to stay in bed or not awaken you in the middle of the night. Just as children require this important developmental stage to help them become mature adults, they also need to be taught skills to handle their fear.

Helping Your Child Handle Fear

When you sense that your child is calling out or getting out of bed because he is genuinely fearful, it's important to recognize and respect that fear. Whatever he is afraid of is *real* to him. Once you've verbally acknowledged to your child that you understand he is afraid, it is then important to help him come up with some things that will help him be less fearful. Let's see how this looks:

Frank's son, Adam, slept peacefully until he was two years old. Then one night, as soon as Frank put him in bed, Adam's eyes got wide. "Daddy! I scared!"

"What are you scared of, Adam?" Frank replied.

"Dogs!" Adam exclaimed.

Frank was puzzled. Adam loved dogs. Though they didn't have one of their own, he usually wanted to pet every one he encountered on the street. He had never expressed fear before.

"Adam, you like dogs. Besides, there are no dogs here. Go to sleep." Frank began to leave the room.

"Daddy!" Adam screamed as tears began to flow. "Doggy! Under bed!"

Suddenly, Frank realized that he wasn't dealing with an actual object that Adam was afraid of, but rather with Adam's fantasy — which, for Adam, was indistinguishable from reality. Frank decided to take a little time and handle this the way he'd been trained to in Active Parenting. He turned, went back to Adam's bed, and sat down.

"You seem really afraid, Adam. Really scared."

Adam nodded, tears still falling. "Scared!" He clutched his father's shirt frantically.

Frank was reassuring. "This house is safe, Adam. I can tell you're scared though. Of dogs?" he questioned.

Adam nodded. "Dogs . . . under bed, Daddy."

"Oh, boy," said Frank. "It must be really scary for you to be so upset. Can you think of anything that would help you feel more safe?"

Adam looked up at his father, but shook his head "no."

"I wonder what would happen if we looked under the bed. Would that help?" Frank questioned. Adam clutched him harder, still shaking his head "no." "Well, what would happen if I called Mommy and she looked. Would that help?" Again, Adam shook his head "no." "Hmmm, must be pretty scary. Can you think of anything that *would* help?" Frank asked. Again, "no."

Frank gently extricated himself from Adam's grasp. "Adam, I can tell you're scared. I want to help. What can I do?" Adam began to cry again. "Nothing!" he replied. "Scared!"

"This house is safe, but I'll tell you what," said his father. "You're good at figuring things out, and I know you'll be able to think of something that will help you feel safe. When you think of it, call me, and I'll come help with whatever it is. Now it's bedtime, and I'm going to leave. But when you think of what will make you not feel so afraid, you call me." And with that, Frank began to leave the room.

"Daddy!" screamed Adam. "Want light!"

Frank turned around. "That's a great idea, Adam. Sounds like you thought of something that will help you feel safer." Adam nodded his head, and Frank went into the hallway to turn on the light. Adam put his head back on his pillow and grabbed his teddy bear.

"Good job, Adam. I'm proud of you for thinking of something that makes you feel better. I'll see you in the morning." And with that, Frank left the room, and Adam fell asleep.

This wasn't the only night that Adam felt afraid. But little by little, as Frank recognized and respected Adam's fear and helped him come up with ways to feel courageous, Adam learned to handle his fear on his own. Within a few months, Adam was again sleeping fearlessly.

How Did This Work?

Frank did several things that expedited this process. Let's look at them one by one:

1) He accepted that Adam was feeling real fear.

2) He reflected Adam's fear back to him. He said, "You seem really afraid, Adam. Really scared." He did not put Adam down for being afraid of nothing.

3) He reassured Adam without denying his fear: "This house is safe, Adam. I can tell you're scared, though. Of dogs?"

4) Instead of giving advice by saying, "Let's look under the bed, and you'll see there aren't any dogs. Then you won't be afraid anymore," he *asked* if looking under the bed would help Adam feel safer. When Adam said it wouldn't, he respected that and explored other possibilities.

5) He didn't indicate by his actions that there was anything to be afraid of — in other words, he didn't play the protector and stay in Adam's room. Had he done so, he might have sent the message that there really *was* something to be afraid of — something Adam couldn't handle on his own.

6) He encouraged his son to come up with ways to handle his own fear — both by helping him explore different solutions to the fear and by ultimately leaving the decision in Adam's hands.

When a child is genuinely afraid, and that fear is interrupting his sleep, it's important to take the time to handle the situation. Ignoring, denying, or making light of the fear will only prolong the process. At the same time, it's also extremely important that we don't allow our children to turn our concern for their fear into an opportunity to manipulate bedtime. We must still be firm about the limits we set, even if it means ultimately leaving the issue of overcoming the fear in the child's hands, as Frank finally did. When you do this, you'll probably find that your child will rise to the challenge and name something that will help him handle nighttime more courageously.

BEDTIME NEEDS

Another reason that children call out in the night is that they haven't yet taken responsibility for satisfying their own needs. For example, as an adult, if your pillow fell out of bed, you might at some point wake up, because you wouldn't be comfortable. Recognizing that the pillow had fallen, you would probably reach down and pick it up, put it under your head, and go back to sleep. A child, however, who has not yet learned to take some responsibility for her own comfort, might call out for Mommy or Daddy to come and get the pillow. Helping our children learn to satisfy their own needs at their level of capability is one of the greater challenges of parenthood.

Satisfying Her Own Needs

When my daughter was three, she slept with a favorite stuffed bear she called Biggie Bear. For several nights in a row, she had been waking up at around 3:00 a.m., because he had fallen out of bed. She would begin to cry and call for either her father or me to come pick him up and put him back in bed, after which she would go right back to sleep.

After the third night, my husband and I were tired. After some discussion, we decided that it was becoming a habit, and it was time to teach her how to take care of some of her own needs. We agreed that the next night we would awaken fully if she called out, and we would be prepared to spend as much time as it took to teach her this vital skill.

That night, when she cried out, we responded verbally instead of with our physical presence:

"What's the matter, honey?" my husband called from our bedroom.

"I want Biggie Bear," she cried.

"Where is Biggie Bear, Em?" I queried.

"On the floor. Biggie Bear! I want Biggie Bear!" She began to cry.

"Sweetheart?" I listened and heard her muffle her crying to listen to me. "Getting Biggie Bear is something you can do."

Her sobs escalated again. "I can't, Mommy! I want *you* to get Biggie Bear. I need Biggie Bear!"

"I know, Em," said her father. "Biggie Bear is important to you. But getting him is something you can do."

"I'm scared, Daddy!" Her sobs were turning into shrieks. "I *can't* get him. I'm scared. Please get him for me, please?"

This kind of exchange went on for some time. It was heartwrenching. She was genuinely upset, but my husband and I had decided that even if it took hours, we were going to get through this tonight. She needed to be able to satisfy her own needs, or we would spend every night getting out of bed to help her.

"Honey? Em?" I listened until I could hear her sobbing quiet and knew she was listening to me. "It's okay that you're scared. Everyone is scared sometimes. And if you're too scared to get Biggie Bear, then that's okay, too. You have a choice. You can either get out of bed and get Biggie Bear, or you can go back to sleep without him. You decide."

She began to cry again. "Mommy, please . . . I want *you* to get him. Please! I'm scared."

"I know, Em," I replied. "I know it can be scary. But you have a choice. You can either go back to sleep without Biggie Bear and get him in the morning, or you can get out of bed and get him. You know what, though? I bet if you get out of bed and get Biggie

Bear, you're going to feel so proud of yourself! And Mommy and Daddy will be proud, too. We know you can do it, Em, and it's your choice. What are you going to choose?"

The crying continued. We waited silently in bed. Slowly, the crying stopped, and for several minutes we thought she'd gone back to sleep. Then we heard some movement. "Mommy?" a little voice said.

"Yes, sweetie?" I replied.

"I'm scared to get Biggie Bear."

"I know, sweetie. It can be scary. I bet if you get him, though, you're going to feel so proud of yourself. What are you going to choose? Do you know?" I could feel my husband holding his breath next to me.

There was silence. It extended for perhaps a minute. Suddenly, the quiet was broken by a joyful shout. "I did it, Mommy! I did it!" she screamed. "I got Biggie Bear! I did it!"

My husband and I shouted, too. "Great, Em! We knew you could do it! I bet you're so proud of yourself. Do you feel proud?"

"Yes!" she exclaimed.

"We're proud of you, too, Em. Really proud. It was hard to get up and get Biggie Bear, but you did it. Good job. We'll see you in the morning."

Emilie replied, "Okay, Mommy."

And with that, we all went back to sleep.

The entire process had taken about fifty minutes. That's a long time — especially at 3 a.m.! The result? We were never awakened at night again in order to get Biggie Bear. Since then, there have been times when I would be on my way to bed and happen into her room in time to see her reach down (still asleep) to pick up her bear. She also covers herself back up during the night if she's cold. In other words, she learned to satisfy her own needs, she achieved some independence, and most importantly, she demonstrated her courage — not only to us, but to herself. And she felt proud!

How It's Done

What are the steps that we took to help her? Let's cover them one at a time:

1) Make the decision to **take the time**. At 3 a.m., the world is blurry, you don't feel focused, and you are probably quicker to anger. Prepare yourself for a night of broken sleep and have a plan ready *before* you are awakened. You'll feel much better about being awake if you know ahead of time that it's going to happen.

2) Be firm about not getting out of bed. Realize how important it is for your child to be able to satisfy her own needs in the middle of the night, and allow her to do just that.

3) Give your child a choice. For example, she can either go without the drink of water or get it herself.

4) Empathize and emphasize. Empathize with your child's feelings, and emphasize that you are confident that she will be able to do it if she decides to.

5) No matter *what* she chooses, give lots of encouragement. Tell her, "I knew you'd be able to make that decision. Good job," even if she chose *not* to get out of bed for the bear or drink of water. Making decisions is difficult, and by encouraging your child's ability to make decisions, you make it easier for her to continue to do so — hopefully without your help at 3 a.m.!

6) Conclude the discussion. When she's made a decision, say, "See you in the morning," so that she will know that her nighttime interaction with Mom and Dad has come to an end.

What If It Doesn't End?

What happens if your child has trouble making a decision? What happens if the discussion goes on and on, beyond what you think is reasonable?

Say, "I know you'll be able to decide, honey, but now it's time for Mommy and Daddy to go back to sleep. We love you, and we'll talk more in the morning." Many times, children will then make a decision quickly, in order to feel as though the matter is closed. Your child might then hop out of bed, grab a drink of water, and say, "I did it!"

It's also possible that she will begin to cry again. If this happens, stick with the "it's time for me to go back to sleep" and remain quiet, unless she specifically engages you again. There is no doubt that you will *not* go back to sleep if she continues to cry, but sometimes crying is part of making a difficult decision.

If she speaks to you again, be firm about reiterating her choice and that it's time for you to go back to sleep. This sounds time-consuming, I know. It sounds as if you could spend the rest of the night awake and interacting with your child. Remember, though, that children often test to see if their parents will be consistent, and it's when parents *aren't* consistent that it takes more time. It's unlikely that, if you remain firm, the behavior will continue for much longer.

In addition, keep in mind that it's the middle of the night for your child, too, and eventually her sleepiness will take over if the matter doesn't get resolved through your interactions.

Your Child's Age And How To Respond

To conclude this chapter, let me take a minute and discuss age-appropriate behavior and bedtime.

INFANCY

I believe in the concept and practice of responding to your infant "on demand." Studies have shown that infants who are picked up when they cry and fed on demand become more secure as toddlers than infants who are required to conform to an adult's routine. I do believe, however, that you can ritualize transitions for your infant just as you can for an older child. Although your infant will initiate the transition, you can have your ritual ready. For example, your child begins crying, because he's hungry. Rather than rush to get the bottle, applesauce, or breast, *speak* to your infant. Say, "I can tell you're hungry. Let's get you something. I'm going to go into the kitchen and get a spoon and the applesauce. Then I'll be back and put you in your chair. When I've opened the lid, it'll be time to eat. Be right back!"

PREVERBAL TODDLERS

This is the ideal period to put into practice your new knowledge of **Preparation and Ritualization**. Beginning the ritual now, including the words, will not only give you practice, but allow your child to get used to a routine prior to the stage in which he begins to resist the sleep transition. Then, when your child finally realizes that the world goes on without him when he's sleeping, you'll have your tools ready, and your structure will be in place to help him more effectively handle bedtime.

VERBAL TODDLERS

It's during this stage that most parents meet with some sort of resistance to their requests that their child go to bed. This is also the time when children are developing their imaginations, and fears about the dark and nighttime set in. If you have not implemented a bedtime ritual before this, do so now! Be sympathetic to your child's needs, while enforcing the limits that are appropriate in your household. The most important qualities you'll need during this period are firmness and confidence. Remember that your child's behavior may get worse initially — remain calm and keep in mind he's only testing you to see if you'll give in. Don't.

SCHOOL-AGE CHILDREN

Resistance to routine and bedtime occurs at this stage as well. Remembering the "work first, play later" philosophy, and ordering events so your child must do the least preferable before the most enjoyable, will help. Keep the traditional parts of the routine your child enjoyed as a toddler, and add a few more that may be more age-appropriate. Ask for your child's help in deciding how the routine should be structured and if he has any suggestions about what to add or take out of the routine. Keep in mind that as the parent, it's your job to enforce the parts of the routine that are important for your child's health, but your child can have a say in the enjoyable parts of the routine.

Plan Ahead

Bedtime resistance, manipulation, and our children's nighttime fears can be some of the greatest frustrations that parents face. They occur when you're tired and want time to yourselves. They occur when you've had a long day, and your normally cooperative child suddenly becomes uncooperative. They occur at three in the morning when you're fast asleep.

Having a ritual and knowing how to prepare your child for sleep can alleviate the anger and frustration that can accompany bedtime. A ritual will not only provide your child with a sense of order, it will provide *you* with one as well. Having a plan to follow if your child gets up after bedtime, or if he's fearful or calls out in the middle of the night, will ease your confusion and frustration. Remember — taking the time to handle upsets ultimately *creates* time, rather than diminishing it.

ELEVEN

UMBRELLAS ON WINDY DAYS

THE POWER OF ENCOURAGEMENT

It was raining. Torrential rain. Buckets of rain. Cats and dogs, as they say. I had to take my daughter, then twenty months old, across town (a thirty minute trip on a nice day) in her stroller, in the rain. Wouldn't you know it, this was also the day *before* we were going to buy the new stroller — the one with the canvas canopy, the one on which you could successfully hang a rain cover, which would have draped gracefully over the stroller like a miniature tent, protecting my daughter fully from the rain. The rain had come one day too early.

The solution to the dilemma was obvious. She would have to carry her umbrella. She had done it before — I knew she was capable — it's just that we'd never gone quite that distance before. Pumping myself full of optimism, I smiled encouragingly at her and explained the situation.

"You'll get to carry your umbrella, sweetheart!" I exclaimed with somewhat false enthusiasm.

"Okay!" *Her* enthusiasm was genuine, at least.

When we got outside, I handed her the umbrella. "Hold tight,

Em," I said. "It's windy out."

It was, too! I considered hailing a taxi, but there were none in sight (of course). I sighed and started out. Twenty steps later, we were about to round the first corner, when WHAP! My face was suddenly full of wet rubber (or latex, or plastic, or whatever those children's umbrellas are made of). Almost letting go of my own umbrella, I caught hers and returned it to her, saying firmly, "Em, you have to hold the umbrella tight. It hit me in the face."

"'Kay!" she replied brightly. We took twelve more steps. WHAP! Rain soaked my shirt where the wet rubber hit.

"Emilie! Hold on to your umbrella! Don't let go!"

"'Kay!" another smile, as she took hold of it once again. Five steps further, WHOOSH! Her umbrella flew past me, leaving its wet imprint on some poor businessman's legs.

"I'm so sorry," I mumbled as he returned the umbrella to me. "So sorry. Thank you so much. I'm sorry." He said nothing, which I considered generous.

What To Do?

As I returned the umbrella to my daughter, I knew that we had a problem, and that something must be done. I decided to give her an "I" message:

"Emilie, when you let go of the umbrella, I feel upset, because it keeps hitting me or someone else. I would like you to hold very tightly to the umbrella from now on."

She nodded seriously. "Okay, Mommy."

There! I felt quite pleased with myself. I hadn't lost my temper, and she'd understood. I'd handled the situation in a mature fashion, as a "good" parent should. I set out again, full of confidence.

We made it two whole steps this time. WHAP!

I steeled myself. Don't get angry, I lectured myself sternly. Maybe she hadn't heard me clearly. I took a deep breath and repeated myself (a bit more firmly than before):

"Emilie, when you let go of the umbrella, I feel angry, because it hits me. I would like you to hold *very* tightly to the umbrella from now on."

This time we made it all the way to the second corner (a half block away), before I had another face full of umbrella. I was beginning to hate wet rubber.

Desperate Measures

Time, I thought, for her to experience the consequences of letting go of her umbrella in the rain. Thus far, only I had experienced them.

"Emilie." I looked at her square in the face. "Either hold on to the umbrella, or I'll fold it and put it away for awhile, and you'll get wet." (It was a warm, summer rain, so I knew she wouldn't get chilled.) She took the umbrella.

We got across the street.

WHAP!

I "calmly" took the umbrella and folded it up, hanging it on the back of the stroller. My daughter began to scream. "Em, I'm really sorry you chose not to hold on to the umbrella. You'll have a chance to try again at the blue awning (a half block away)." I walked shakily towards the blue awning.

At this point I was now wet, angry, and being stared at by every person within earshot. Somehow I persisted, and we made it to the blue awning. As I unfolded my daughter's umbrella, I said, "Em, remember, you have a choice. You can either hold on to the umbrella without letting go, or you can have me fold it up and hang it on the back of the stroller."

She nodded, gripping the umbrella. We didn't even make it to the end of the block before the umbrella was again folded and hung up, my daughter screaming once again. I was discouraged, she was discouraged, and we were still only a few blocks from home, having taken twenty minutes to get that far.

I told her she could try again once we got across the street. I needed time to think. I'd given her an "I" message, so she knew what all this was about and how I felt. She'd experienced the consequences of her decision to let go of the umbrella and gotten wet. But no progress had been made. We were both wet, angry, and at this rate, a good forty minutes away from our destination.

When All Else Fails

Suddenly, something clicked in my head. I knew it might be a long-shot, but I had just taught a class on the value of encouragement and wondered if, perhaps, that might be the key.

We got across the street, and I unfolded and gave the umbrella back. As I handed it to Emilie, I said, "Em, I know it's hard, but I also know you'll be able to hold on to the umbrella and not let go." She looked up at me with wide eyes, and I smiled (though shakily) at her. I straightened up, got behind the stroller and took one step. Then I knelt down and looked at her, smiling. "Good job, Em! You held on to the umbrella, I'm proud of you." Her face registered surprise. I stood up again. We took two steps this time, when I knelt down beside her and gave her another smile. "Em," I said, "I'm so proud of you! I knew you could do it. Good for you for holding on to the umbrella so tight!" Her face broadened into a big smile, and I smiled back. "You're terrific at holding that umbrella, sweetie. Thanks!" I stood again, and we walked the rest of the way across town. From that point on, she never once let go of the umbrella. Not that time, nor any time since.

A Little Goes A Long Way

This story illustrates the power of encouragement. It also says a lot about the lasting effect that a little encouragement can have on behavior.

It's important to note that encouragement is an ongoing process. You can do this by having positive expectations about things that you know your child is capable of at her age, and by giving her praise for the little steps she takes towards accomplishing various tasks.

Expectations

Whenever I tell this story in my class on encouragement, I'm almost always asked the same question: "Weren't you expecting too much from a twenty-month-old? My daughter/son, wouldn't have been able to do that. Isn't it discouraging to expect so much from your child?"

The answer is two-fold:

1) If you expect too much from your child — for example, expecting them to begin reading at age two and pushing them in that direction — then *yes*! It *is* discouraging, and maybe even damaging. The key is in knowing where your child is developmentally and what she's capable of. You can learn this by reading about child development and age-appropriate skills and tasks, and (perhaps more importantly) by spending time with your child, so that you know what her individual capabilities are.

2) Was I expecting too much from *my* child? The answer is, based on the outcome, no. With a little encouragement, she was obviously capable of holding on to the umbrella, even on a windy day. But I knew this beforehand. I had already seen that she had the strength to carry an umbrella and knew she was capable of understanding and accepting the consequences of her behavior. Had I continued on a disciplinary tact, however, with different logical consequences and more "I" messages, then yes, it could have been discouraging for her. In this case, she wasn't purposely letting go of the umbrella and testing limits. The wind was rather strong, and I came to realize that she needed, instead

of discipline, a strengthening of her internal motivation for keeping a tight grasp. Encouragement gave her that motivation.

Why Not Skip The Preliminaries?

Another question I am invariably asked is, "Why didn't you just use the encouragement, and skip the "I" message and logical consequence altogether? Wouldn't that have taken care of the problem sooner?"

The answer to this question is, "Maybe." The fact is, even though I'm a parent educator, I'm also human, and I, like you, don't always know all the answers. In addition, I sometimes make mistakes. Many times, it takes me a couple of tries before I hit on what my child really needs in a particular situation.

Making Mistakes

To help you learn, I'll tell you about the mistakes I made that day. But before I do, let me first tell you a few things about mistakes in general. These are truths that you should hold dear as you face the many frustrations of being a parent. If you take these truths about mistakes to heart and hold them close, you'll find the journey you are on as a parent smoothed by confidence, instead of bumpy from guilt and worry.

About mistakes:

1) Mistakes are for learning. They help us test our knowledge, and they can help us to become more effective in dealing with our children. By analyzing what we did "wrong," we can figure out how to do things differently the next time.

2) We are human. We are not perfect. And as parents, perfection is *not* something we want to strive for — if we were to somehow achieve it, where would that leave our children? Perfection is too difficult to live up to, and we need to give

our children obtainable goals, not unrealistic ones.

Finally,

3) It's not necessarily what you do or say, it's what you do or say *after* what you've already done or said. If you make a mistake, your child can learn a valuable lesson by your willingness to admit the mistake and try it a different way. At age four, my daughter, after having yelled at me or thrown a tantrum of some sort, would come back with no prompting on my part and say, "I'm sorry I yelled at you. I could have done it differently. I'll try to talk next time instead."

The Mistakes I Made

With this knowledge about the value of mistakes, let me tell you about the ones I made on that windy, rainy day.

First of all, I didn't give my daughter the "I" message soon enough. By saying things such as "Don't let go" and "You've got to hold the umbrella tight, it hit me in the face," I was actually discouraging her. Almost any sentence that begins with the word "don't" has the hidden meaning, "I expect you to." So by saying "Don't let go," I was in effect saying, "I expect you to let go, so *don't do it!*" In addition, by delaying the "I" message, I allowed my anger to build, which made it difficult for me to think clearly and caused my tone of voice to become irritated and sound threatening. When children feel discouraged, as mine obviously did, it makes it difficult for them to carry out the tasks they might normally accomplish with ease. Once my child felt *encouraged*, her behavior changed, and she completed the task successfully.

The second mistake I made was in repeating the "I" message. While I may have done so with good intentions, such as believing that she didn't hear me, repetition allowed my frustration to build, and I became discouraging, rather than encouraging. "I" messages work best if they're said once, then followed by a logical consequence (also spoken only one time), and ultimately followed by an action on the part of the parent. Repetition only makes the parent frustrated and gives the child the message that the parent doesn't really mean what they say.

What I Did Right

Now, to end this chapter appropriately, I cannot conclude with my mistakes. Just as I would encourage you to do when analyzing a situation with your child, I must balance my analysis of my mistakes with my knowledge of the things I did right. After all, parents need encouragement, too!

Trying the "I" message first, before encouragement, may have slowed the process some, but it certainly didn't do any damage. In fact, it gave me some practice, and because my feelings were engaged, it *was* the right way to start. I simply could have dropped it sooner than I did.

Allowing my child to "try again" provided the opportunity for her to develop responsibility. A child who is not allowed to try again with the same situation never has a chance to put into practice what she has learned from the consequences that she experienced. Because Emilie was young, I gave her the opportunity to try again relatively quickly. Had she been older, I would have allowed more time between tries.

And when I finally decided to try encouragement instead of discipline with my child, I knew that I needed to catch her in the act of doing it right. I was aware from experience that it might only be a split second — one footstep on that long journey across town — in which she'd be holding on to that umbrella tightly. I realized that I had to seize that moment and glorify it. And that's exactly what I did. By encouraging the "baby steps," I empowered her to continue to hold on to that umbrella for the remainder of the journey.

When you catch your children in the act of doing something right, you have a golden opportunity to motivate them and allow them to feel proud of themselves. Catch your child in the act — the act of doing it *right* — and seize the moment!

TWELVE

MELTING CHILDREN

THE ART OF THE TANTRUM

I was walking through a grocery store, when a mother and her five-year-old son caught my eye. They were in the produce section, and I noticed them right away because of the slightly wild cast in the mother's eye. She looked like a fox trapped by hunting dogs. Trying not to stare, I moved a bit closer and could hear that, although her breath was slightly ragged, she was making a valiant attempt to remain calm and keep her voice low. "Good for you, Mom!" I thought. In a few short moments, while I pretended to be inspecting apples, it became clear to me that mother and son were involved in a battle of wills. She wanted to get the shopping done quickly and was requesting that he sit in the cart instead of walking, and he, knowing that he had something that she wanted (and therefore had the upper hand), was negotiating for some sort of treat before he would comply with her request. When I arrived, Mom was in the middle of attempting to reason with her son. The conversation went something like this:

Mom: "Honey, I need to get out of here quickly. Please sit in the cart."

Son: "I want a treat."

Mom: "I have an idea! Why don't you ride on the side of the cart, standing and holding on!" (By the way, a dangerous thing to do.)

Son: "Please, Mommy, can I have a treat?"

Mom: "Honey, we have to get to Grandma's house by two. It's ten minutes after one, and we haven't finished half of our shopping. I need your help."

Son: "I want a treat."

Mom: "Johnny, you just had a treat at lunch. We have to leave soon. Grandma's expecting us. Please hold on to the side of the cart. You *like* to ride on the side of the cart."

Son: "But I want *another* treat! I *won't* ride in the cart if you don't give me a treat!"

The conversation had gone from difficult to worse! There is nothing like a child's ultimatum to push Mom or Dad over the edge. I held my breath and waited anxiously to see what would happen next.

Mom strode to her son and reached down to pick him up. She had obviously decided that talk wasn't working and she needed to try action. As she placed her hands under his arms and began to lift, I witnessed one of the most extraordinary phenomena known to parents — the melting child! Johnny suddenly went limp, his arms pointed floppily towards the heavens, and he literally melted out of her hands and onto the floor. Though the phenomenon has not yet been validated by science, I also knew, through experience, that Johnny's body was now over triple its former weight, and that even a crane couldn't lift the puddle of child flesh from the floor.

As Mom began to talk once again, I walked away, knowing that she had already lost the battle.

The mother in the grocery store experienced what all parents experience at one point or another — her child threw a tantrum.

What Is A Tantrum?

"A tantrum!" you might be saying to yourself. "*That* wasn't a tantrum! A tantrum is when my child throws himself to the floor, kicks and screams, and embarrasses me."

You would be right. Kicking and screaming are *one type* of tantrum. But there are other kinds as well, and in this chapter, I'll give you step-by-step instructions on how to identify and handle the different tantrum types. Be aware as you're reading that, for the sake of clarity, the examples given are simplified. If your child throws a tantrum, and in following the appropriate steps, you find that you aren't conquering the tantrum, try labeling it differently and using another technique. Always remember that the techniques and skills presented throughout this book are like a bag of tools. You may begin thinking you need a screwdriver from your bag, then you examine the problem more closely and decide you need a wrench instead. Feel comfortable trying the different techniques as you begin to diminish the tantrums your child throws.

IDENTIFYING TANTRUM TYPES

As I mentioned above, tantrums can take different forms. These differences can be categorized into **three basic tantrum types**. How we handle tantrums effectively is based upon what type of tantrum it is.

The Frustrated Tantrum

We'll begin by differentiating the first type of tantrum — the **Frustrated Tantrum**.

The Frustrated Tantrum generally occurs when your child is about to enter a new developmental stage. It gets its name not from the parent's feelings of frustration, but from the child's.

This type of tantrum occurs because children often understand what they want before they are either physically or mentally capable of achieving their goal. For example, a child may understand the concept of holding an object before he is capable of actually reaching out for that object. This results in what I call "developmental frustration," and this type of frustration occurs throughout your child's life.

For the infant and toddler, the stages of crawling, walking, and talking can be the source of frustration and "tantruming." For the school-age child, learning the skills necessary for schoolwork may cause frustration — writing, reading, even socializing with other children. Even during adolescence, there is potential for Frustrated Tantrums, because of hormonal changes, separation issues, and the adolescent's need to reconcile independence with dependence.

Before I give you the tools necessary to handle this type of tantrum, let's first take a look at the other two types.

The Escalated Tantrum

The second type of tantrum, the **Escalated Tantrum**, generally occurs when your agenda conflicts with your child's. It looks something like this:

Dad: "Come on, it's time to go. Put your coat on."

Daughter: (No response)

Dad (More forcefully): "Ginny, it's time to go. Put your coat on."

Daughter (In a whiney voice): "Just one more . . . (cartoon, bite of food, sip of juice . . . whatever)."

Dad: "No, we've got to go. Come on."

Daughter: "I don't wanna!"

Dad (Trying to get the child's arm into the sleeve): "Put your coat on!"

Daughter: "Noooooooooooo!"

The Escalated Tantrum usually ends with the parent attempting to physically control the child in some way, either by picking her up, dragging her by the hand, or as in the case above, trying to force the child's arm into the sleeve of her coat.

Johnny, in the grocery store at the beginning of this chapter, was engaged in an Escalated Tantrum. I call it escalated, not because of the way it ends, but because of how it progresses. The child becomes more and more resistant to the parent's demands, digging his heels in deeper each step of the way. Johnny simply chose to passively resist (by melting) at the end of the scene, instead of actively resisting (by screaming and kicking). In the end, Johnny's mother attempted to physically control him.

It's important to recognize that you cannot control your children unless you're strong enough to physically restrain them or pick them up. Even then, you're only able to *physically* control them. How much better it is to rely upon techniques and tools that will engage your children in *cooperating* with you instead of simply bowing down to your (sometimes) larger physical structure. When you recognize that even with superior physical strength you cannot ultimately control your children, you'll rely more on the techniques and tools given in this book and become, in the end, more resourceful and more effective as a parent.

The Manipulative Tantrum

The third type of tantrum is what I call the **Manipulative Tantrum**. The Manipulative Tantrum generally occurs when you have already enforced some type of discipline or decision with your child. It's based on your child's belief that, "If I scream long and hard enough, Mom/Dad will change their mind." Again, how you handle this type of tantrum will differ from your handling of the other two.

How Do You Handle Tantrums?

There are two steps to handling tantrums, no matter what type they are:

1) Handling your thoughts and feelings

2) Formulating and carrying out a plan of action

STEP 1: HANDLING THOUGHTS AND FEELINGS

The first step, **handling your thoughts and feelings**, is the same for any type of tantrum. In almost any tantrum situation, Mom or Dad generally feels out of control. This loss of control adds to your child's tantrum. When children themselves lose control, the thing they need the most is a parent who is *in* control.

But how do we gain control in a tantrum situation, when our feelings become so quickly engaged? To understand how to do this, remember the THINK, FEEL, DO cycle you learned about in Chapter Eight. Remembering that our thoughts cause our feelings, try to identify the negative thoughts that are causing the negative feelings that get in the way of your taking positive action (the DO part of the cycle).

For example, let's say that you're Johnny's mother in the grocery store. What are your thoughts? Maybe you're thinking things such as: "I can't stand for things to go wrong," "This is awful," "My mother will be furious if we're late," "Everyone is looking at me," "I don't know what to do," "This always happens," "Someone is going to take my child away from me," "I'm not a good parent," or "I'm not in control."

The first step when any tantrum begins is to take charge of

these thoughts. You must feel a sense of control in order to initiate Step Two in handling a tantrum: forming an Action Plan. And in order to feel a sense of control, you must think thoughts that provoke either neutral or positive feelings.

With this in mind, what thoughts could you think that would help you feel calmer, not so embarrassed?

Maybe you could think some of the following things:

* "I don't like it, but I can stand it."
* "This is a problem, but I can handle it."
* "Everyone's child has tantrums."
* "I can handle it when things go wrong."
* "I'd like this to happen less."
* "I feel so sorry for my child."
* "Seems like s/he's having a tough time."
* "I am a good parent."
* "I am in control."
* "No one has the right to judge my effectiveness as a parent but me."
* "Boy, this is a big one!"

When I initially teach this thought pattern change to parents, I ask that they memorize the positive phrases above. Because you can only think one thought at a time, if you adopt one of these and repeat it over and over, you can, quite literally, shove the automatic, negative thoughts from your head. Parents are often amazed at the difference it makes to use one of these phrases instead of reverting to their normal pattern. Once they begin to use positive thinking, their feelings change as well, and they begin to feel capable, confident, and calm. Sometimes they can even see a little humor in the situation. And because feelings cause us to take action, if you remain calm, you will then be able to formulate your Action Plan, which is the next step in handling tantrums (the DO part of the cycle).

A Brief Review

Before continuing with what you will DO, let's briefly review what's going to happen the next time your child has a tantrum. When the tantrum begins, you will think two things to yourself:

1) Is this a Frustrated, Escalated or Manipulative Tantrum?

And after you've identified the type, think:

2) I know exactly how to handle this. Things are under control. (Or one of the other positive phrases mentioned above. Repeat it over and over if necessary.)

STEP 2: THE ACTION PLAN

Now you're ready to think about how you *are* going to handle the tantrum. This is the DO part of the cycle. It is your **Action Plan**, which will differ according to the type of tantrum you identified.

The Frustrated Tantrum Action Plan

This is the tantrum that occurs when your child is frustrated about something he is doing or trying to do.

To understand frustration from your child's point of view, let's think for a moment about his THINK, FEEL, DO cycle:

Event: Your three-year-old is trying to get the top off a plastic jar.

HIS THOUGHT: "I know this comes off, I've seen Mommy/Daddy do it," followed by, "It's not coming off. I can't get it off."

HIS FEELING: Frustration.

HIS ACTION: Banging, throwing, screaming — something along those lines — resulting in a tantrum, of course!

The tantrum has been set off by the **negative** thoughts in your child's cycle.

Your Action Plan for the Frustrated Tantrum, therefore, will involve helping your child think **positively** instead of negatively. This includes three steps:

1) Getting three "yes's."

2) Supporting positive thoughts.

3) Thinking of positive DO's.

STEP 1: GETTING THREE "YES'S"

The object of Step One is to acknowledge and, therefore, validate your child's feelings at least three times. This will help your child become calmer, he will feel as though you understand him, and eventually, he will learn to label his own emotions and communicate his frustration with words, not tantrums.

Step One sounds like this:

"You seem really frustrated."

"That's a really hard top to get off. It made you angry when it wouldn't come off."

"You were so angry that you . . . (threw it, banged it, screamed)."

The "three yes's" refers to getting your child's acknowledgement that you understand his feelings **three times**. Until you've gotten three yes's, don't go on to Step Two. This may take awhile, and you may get a few no's in the meantime, but that's okay. Keep trying — it'll be worth it in the end. In fact, many times, just getting the three yes's will stop the tantrum!

If the child is too young to acknowledge you verbally, then look for physical cues that would indicate you're on the right track: a lessening of tears, a sudden clinging to you, an attentiveness in his facial expression that wasn't there before. Because you will be looking for nonverbal cues, however, go for five yes's instead of three.

THINGS TO LOOK OUT FOR

Before we go on to Step Two, let me add a few cautionary words about Step One in this Action Plan:

1) Don't add "buts." For example: *"But* you'll understand how to get the top off some day" or *"But* you'll get over it." This will only communicate to your child that you don't *really* understand how he feels at all. You must give the message that you truly understand how hard it is. If your child feels misunderstood, it only prolongs the tantrum.

2) What do you do if your child continues to scream? Many parents tell me that during a tantrum, their child is screaming too loudly to hear them. If the parent believes (the THINK part of the cycle) that their child isn't listening, what feeling would the parent have? Probably helplessness. What kind of action (the DO part of the cycle) would the parent then take if he feels helpless? Well, a helpless parent might give up or try to scream above the child. It is therefore imperative, even if you think your child cannot hear you, that you *keep your tone of voice level and talk through the screaming.* Assume that your child hears and understands you so you don't get caught in your own negative cycle. Otherwise, it will be very difficult to support your child in thinking positively — Step Two in

your Action Plan for the Frustrated Tantrum.

STEP 2: SUPPORTING POSITIVE THOUGHTS

Just like changing your thoughts in your own THINK, FEEL, DO cycle, you can support your child in changing his thoughts.

This is done by verbally showing confidence in your child's abilities. In order to know what to say, put yourself in your child's shoes. What are some of the negative thoughts you might have if you couldn't get the lid off a jar? How can you substitute positive thoughts for these negative ones? More importantly, how can you communicate these positive alternatives to your child?

Your supportive communication might look like this:

CHILD'S NEGATIVE THOUGHT	YOUR SUPPORTIVE COMMUNICATION
"I can't do it."	"It *is* a really hard top to get off. I'll bet you can do it though."
"This is too hard!"	"Sometimes it takes a few tries."
"I hate this, I'll never get it!"	"Sticky lids can be frustrating."

STEP THREE: INITIATING ACTION

Finally, after acknowledging and validating your child's feelings about the task and encouraging your child to think positively, the third step in your Action Plan will be to help your child think of positive DO's.

Positive action alternatives are communicated to your child like this:

"Let's try it together."

"Next time, ask me, and we'll work it out together."

"I wonder if there is anything you can do?"

"How can I help?"

I especially encourage parents to choose the latter two responses. When we support our children in solving their *own* problems and allow them the opportunity to come up with their own positive alternatives under our guidance, we give them a valuable tool that they'll take with them into adulthood.

The Escalated Tantrum Action Plan

The Escalated Tantrum occurs when your child's agenda conflicts with yours. It frequently ends with the parent attempting to physically control the child in some way.

There are two parts to the Escalated Tantrum Action Plan:

1) An explanation
2) An action

STEP 1: THE EXPLANATION

In this case, we precede action with an explanation for two reasons. First, we want our children to understand that having a tantrum is a choice, and like all choices, it has consequences. It is important, therefore, that we make a brief statement to the child that will connect her choices with the consequences that will follow (our action). Second, by preceding actions with words, we give our child the chance to correct her behavior based on what we say, not always on what we do.

Because this initial explanation is concise and follows a specific form, it can be differentiated from reasoning with your child. Many parents have come to me and said, "But I've tried reasoning, and it doesn't work." They're right! Reasoning with your child doesn't work, because a child reasons in a different way from an adult. Children aren't capable of reasoning the way adults do until they *become adults*. This doesn't mean, however, that our children aren't entitled to an explanation of why their actions have consequences. So it's important that the explanation — an amended "I" message — be concise, have a format, and be stated *only once* to the child.

THE AMENDED "I" MESSAGE

Here's what the format for the amended "I" message looks like:

When you_____,

I feel_____,

because_____.

Either_____ or _____.

Giving the child a choice at the end of the "I" message often helps break the cycle by directing his focus to the alternatives. In addition, it gives the child some limited power, which often helps him feel in control again.

Here's what an amended "I" message might look like for a child who is refusing to put his coat on in the morning:

When you delay putting on your coat in the morning,

I feel frustrated,

because it slows us down.

Either put your coat on **or** I'll carry you out of the house without it.

OFFERING CHOICES

It's important to keep in mind the following hints about the choices you offer:

1) The choices should be logically related — to each other and to the tantrum. They are not meant to serve as distraction or punishment, but as focus.

2) The choice you give must be something that you can carry through, should the child continue to tantrum. In other words, if your child weighs 85 pounds and you weigh 100 pounds, don't give the child a choice about carrying him out without the coat — you won't be able to enforce that choice, and it will become an empty threat. Instead, you might want to say, "Either put your coat on without fighting, or we won't go out." Or, if you are going to work and will be late, you might want to say, "Either put your coat on without fighting, or tomorrow we'll get up extra early to allow for the time it will take us to fight about this." While this last suggestion may not get you to work on time that day, a few days of being dragged out of bed early will probably change your child's mind about the coat tantrum.

It Takes So Long!

It's important to realize that while the techniques given in this book may take time to begin with, in the long run your child will misbehave less often, and you will teach your child some very important things about cooperation, respect, and responsibility along the way.

Step 2: The Action

Step Two in the Escalated Tantrum Action Plan: the action.

While the amended "I" message alone might stop the tantrum, it's wise to be prepared for Step Two. Children often learn more from actions than from words, so it's important to make the choice something you can (and will!) act upon.

In the example above, the action would be to immediately pick your child up and carry him out.

Don't delay this last step, even if you're unsure as to whether your child heard you or not. You can always reiterate as you're walking out the door — with Escalated Tantrums, action is essential.

The Manipulative Tantrum Action Plan

If you have disciplined your child, or enforced a limit such as bedtime, and she is screaming her head off (this may be after you've acted on the Escalated Tantrum), the only rule is to *sympathize*.

To continue the example above, here's what that would sound like:

> "Gee, I'm really sorry you chose to have me carry you out without your coat."

This should be followed by an explanation that she'll have a chance to try again, giving her a specific time. For small children, trying again may occur in a few minutes. For older children, trying again may be tomorrow. Don't forget that allowing your child to try again helps develop responsibility. It gives them the opportunity to think about how they will handle the same situation next time. In addition, it helps them think positively (the THINK part of the cycle again) if they know they'll have a second chance.

AN ESCALATED-MANIPULATIVE TANTRUM

When my daughter was two-and-a-half, she went through a "no-coat" phase. Every morning, I'd ask her to put her coat on. She'd refuse. I'd explain that it was cold out. She'd refuse. I'd try to grab her to force her coat on. She'd begin to scream. Finally, I handled her Escalated Tantrum in the way described above, by giving her an "I" message with a choice attached — either put the coat on, or I'd carry her out without it. Lost in her drama by this time, she'd forgotten that going out without the coat was what she had actually been asking for (I'd forgotten, too!), and she became incensed that I would ask her to choose anything, much less enforce that choice by carrying her out the door without her coat on. When I acted upon her "non-choice" by scooping her up and leaving (I picked up the coat in my other arm), it caused her to redouble her efforts — the screams became louder as we went down the stairs. I said, "Sounds like you're really angry that you chose to have me carry you out without your coat on. You'll have a chance to try again at the end of the block." Once outside, having discovered how chilly it was, she was happy to don the coat at the corner, and the no-coat tantrums ceased (for *that* winter at least!).

WHAT IF YOUR CHILD *WON'T* CHOOSE?

This raises a question about "non-choices." What do you do about a child who won't choose? The answer is that refusing to choose is a choice! In the adult world, when we refuse to make a choice, very often that choice will be made for us. The same will apply for your child. If she refuses to choose, you can even say, "I see it's hard to choose. If you can't choose, I'll choose for you, and I'll choose _____ (telling them what action you will carry through with if they refuse to choose)."

A SIMPLE MANIPULATIVE TANTRUM

If the Manipulative Tantrum occurs because of a decision you've made (such as no candy until after dinner or that it's time for bed) and not as a result of the Escalated Tantrum, the rule is still to sympathize, but this time you don't need to "try again."

It might sound something like this:

> "Gee, I'm really sorry you're having such a hard time. When you're calmer, we'll talk about the problem."

You can even be more specific if you like:

> "It's hard to wait until after dinner to have candy, isn't it? Sometimes I hate waiting, too. Can you think of anything that would keep you busy while you're waiting?"

Sometimes, focusing the child's attention on what she can do to help herself through the frustration will enable her to break into the action portion of her THINK, FEEL, DO cycle with a positive alternative to her whining or screaming. If, however, your child continues to whine or cry, recognize *that* as a choice she can make, and allow her to be miserable if she wants to. It might mean leaving the room so it doesn't affect your mood, but remember that often a gentle reminder about how she's handling the situation will change even that:

> "I know it's hard. But candy is not allowed until after dinner. I'm sorry you're so unhappy about it, and being unhappy is something you can choose. If you continue to whine, though, I'm going to go into the other room, because I need a little quiet time."

Often, this type of statement will put an end to the manipulation — but *only if you don't give in* to the whining!!! Being firm is crucial to the Action Plan for the Manipulative Tantrum.

Some Final Hints

A few final hints about tantrums in general:

1) If you're in doubt as to the type of tantrum, assume it's a Frustrated Tantrum and use that Action Plan first. If the tantrum continues and you feel your temper coming into play, move immediately to the Action Plan for the Escalated Tantrum.

2) If your child has a tantrum because of another child, even if you saw it *escalate*, use the Frustrated Tantrum Action Plan, unless the situation is dangerous. In case of danger, remove your child immediately, and follow up your actions with an explanation to your child.

Spending Time = Saving Time

Tantrums are a challenge to any parent. Because they take different forms and can occur throughout your child's development, they require the extra attention necessary to learn the skills that will diminish them. This extra attention is well worth it, however, as one parent's story will show:

Garrett's Escalated Tantrums had almost gotten the best of his Mom. Every day it seemed that it was something new. No matter what his Mom, Jane, suggested, the answer was always an emphatic "no" from Garrett. She would wheedle, she would reason, she would get angry. But Garrett always whined louder, demanded more, and screamed louder. The scene always ended with Jane dragging him, physically forcing him, or throwing up her hands in disgust. I suggested that instead of reasoning, she use the steps for the Escalated Tantrum. Weary and defeated, she was ready to try anything. As Jane said, "Anything would be better than what we have now." One week later, she came back with a smiling face and a wonderful success story:

During the week, Jane had given Garrett, then two years old, some juice, the kind that comes in a box with a straw attached. She had warned him, "Don't squeeze the box, Garrett, or the juice will squirt out on the rug." Immediately, Garrett squeezed the box.

Jane was livid. "Garrett! I asked you not to do that, please. Go get a sponge and clean it up."

I'm sure that you can guess what Garrett's reply was!

"No!" he screamed, squeezing the box once more.

Suddenly, Jane remembered our talk. She took a deep breath and said to herself, "Everyone's child has tantrums. I can handle this." Then, turning to her son, she said calmly, "Garrett, when you squeeze juice out on purpose, I feel upset, because it makes a mess and could stain. Either clean the juice up now or put the juice box away."

Garrett looked at her in astonishment. "Away," he replied, still looking shocked.

Surprised herself, Jane said, "Fine, you'll have a chance to try again later," and she took the box and put it in the refrigerator. Then, as she went to get a sponge to clean up the spilled juice, she heard Garrett's small voice behind her: "I'll clean up, Mommy."

Turning around, she knelt and gave Garrett a big hug. "Thank you, Garrett, let's do it together." And with that, a potential tantrum was turned into a loving moment for mother and son.

But the story doesn't end here, although it could and it would still be wonderful and astonishing.

Later, when Jane gave Garrett a chance to "try again," she handed him the juice box and said, "Remember, Garrett, the juice stays in the box, not on the floor."

Garrett, carefully taking the box from her, replied "I know, Mommy. Otherwise, I either clean it up or put it away."

This dramatic success story illustrates the power of the technique that Jane used. It should be mentioned, however, that though encouraging, it didn't mean that Garrett never had another tantrum. Behavior that has taken time to develop often takes awhile to change as well. But for Jane and Garrett, this was clearly a turning point in their relationship, and the beginning of the end of Garrett's tantrums.

For Jane and Garrett, the either/or choice broke the cycle when Garrett made a choice. But what would have happened if Garrett had ignored his Mom and continued squeezing the juice box? As you already know from reading about choices, Mom would have to make a choice for him — and then enforce that choice. Since it would be difficult to force him to clean up the juice, Mom should choose that it be put away, and gently, but firmly take the box from Garrett.

Your own successes may be smaller, larger, or exactly the same as Jane and Garrett's. You may have immediate, dramatic successes, or more gradual, subtle ones. The important thing to keep in mind is that even small successes count, and if you remain confident that the techniques will work, and you work at them calmly and with diligence, you'll change forever the former battleground of your home and achieve a solid foundation for peace.

THIRTEEN

CONSISTENCY, RESPECT, AND THE PICTURE PERFECT PARENT

TYING IT ALL TOGETHER

As you've progressed through this book, you've learned that there are alternatives to the instinctual reactions that most parents have when interacting with their children. I believe that in using these techniques and skills, you will not only become a calmer, more confident parent, but you will also instill in your children the important qualities they need to interact in this increasingly complex society.

In concluding this book, I'd like to leave you with what I consider the two most important skills that I would like to see you acquire — skills that will guide you appropriately in all your interactions with your children. It is these two things that will make your journey easier and your relationship with your children more effective and productive, and ultimately more joyful, as you continue to grow as a parent.

The two most important foundations you can develop as a parent are **respect** and **consistency**.

Respect

Many times we forget this basic, yet essential attitude when we speak to and with our children. We somehow believe that just because they are smaller and not as experienced, that it gives us the right to belittle, berate, or ignore them. While children lack the experience of adults, they are human beings. As such, they have a right to their feelings. Their needs are much like those of adults, and while they are still growing — emotionally, physically, and socially — they have the right to be respected in this process.

Acting respectful towards your child will make her more responsive towards you and, in general, do more to make life easier for you than anything else. It will keep you from having to carry around 3 x 5 cards with techniques written on them, ready to pull out at a moment's notice, because many times being respectful will accomplish your goal all by itself. And when you do use the techniques presented in this book, a respectful attitude will make them work 100 percent more effectively.

The key to maintaining a respectful attitude is no mystery. Simply ask yourself this question: "Would I treat my best friend this way?" This one question will keep your interactions with your child respectful — even when you're angry with each other.

Our immediate family members, those who live with us, are often the people we care most about in the entire world. They provide us with support when we are in need, take care of us when we are ill, listen to us when we have concerns. In addition, they are often seen by us almost as extensions of ourselves — losing one would be like losing an arm or a leg. Yet with all the love we have for them, and the love we receive from them, we often treat them in ways that we wouldn't treat a stranger on the street.

Respecting our children means treating them as we would a precious jewel. And at least giving them the same courtesy that we would give to a guest in our home.

Consistency

The other thing that will make your journey as a parent easier is consistency. Some parent educators are afraid to use the word "consistency" for fear that parents will believe the task is Herculean, and that they will have to be "picture parents." In order to be consistent, we must understand what it is. And to understand what it *is*, we must first understand what it is *not*.

Consistency is *not* being picture perfect. It is *not* always doing the right thing at the right time. When I tell you that you must be consistent as parents, I am not trying to imply that you may never make a mistake or your children will continue to misbehave or be scarred for life.

Consistency *is* having a foundation of techniques and skills on which you can rely in those inevitable moments of crisis. You don't need to be consistent in the way you *feel*; you do need to be consistent in what you *do*. Consistency means using your techniques on a regular basis — not only in crisis, but in your daily living. Consistency is also acting cooperatively with your spouse, so that your child doesn't run to Mom when he doesn't get the answer he wants from Dad. When you deal with your children consistently, you will help them feel safe and secure as they explore the parameters within which they must live.

When parents don't have a foundation upon which to rely, they *can't* be consistent, because they are constantly relying on their "instincts" on the spur of the moment. Unfortunately, as parents, we are almost never sure that our instincts are correct. When one of our children has been screaming for ten minutes, our instincts become subject to all kinds of doubts, and we begin to feel guilty. We wonder, "Am I doing the right thing? Would my child be in so much pain if I were?" It is these doubts that cause us to waver. And in wavering, we become ineffective as parents — we are no longer the leaders and teachers our children need us to be.

Knowing Your Purpose

Parents must have an underlying philosophy — that is, a knowledge of what their **purpose** is as parents — and they must combine that philosophy with a technical foundation on which they can rely. It is then that they will become consistent. When consistency is combined with respect for our children as individuals, we are creating children who will be able to face the adult world with resources that will help them not only to cope, but to thrive.

Parents who are willing to read and train themselves for the important job of being parents, who are willing to admit that they may not know everything, and to admit that instinct isn't enough, will create children who are responsible not only to others, but to themselves, and who will feel comfortable working with others to achieve common goals. In other words, your children will be interdependent, not simply dependent or independent. It is your children who will grow up feeling that they have a voice. It is your children who will have the vision, insight, and courage to make needed changes in the world when they become adults. And because you had the courage to educate yourself for parenthood, your children will not only have vision and insight, but will have the capability and resources to implement their vision.

It takes guts to throw away instinct. Congratulations!

APPENDIX

EIGHT DO'S OF LOGICAL CONSEQUENCES

1) Give the child a choice:
   - either/or
   - when/then
2) Make sure the consequence is logical.
3) Ask the child to help.
4) Give choices that you can live with.
5) Keep your tone firm and friendly.
6) Give the choice only once, then act.
7) Expect testing.
8) Allow the child to try again later.

From Popkin, Michael H., Ph.D. *Active Parenting: Teaching Cooperation, Courage and Responsibility.* San Francisco: Harper San Francisco, 1987.

REFERENCES

PREFACE

1. Shorter, Edward. *The Making of the Modern Family.* New York: Basic Books, Inc., 1977.

2. Miller, Alice. *For Your Own Good: Hidden cruelty in child-rearing and the roots of violence.* New York: Farrar, Straus, Giroux, 1984.

3. Clarke, Jean Illsley. *Self-Esteem: A Family Affair.* New York: Harper & Row, 1980; and Dawson, Connie. *Growing Up Again.* New York: Harper & Row, 1989; as quoted in Bradshaw, John. *Homecoming: Reclaiming and Championing Your Inner Child.* New York: Bantam Books, 1990.

CHAPTER ONE

4. Covey, Stephen R. *The 7 Habits of Highly Effective People: Powerful Lessons in Personal Change.* New York: Simon & Schuster, Inc., 1990.

CHAPTERS FOUR AND SIX

5. *Active Parenting Today* is a video-based parenting program developed by Dr. Michael Popkin. For further information, see page 148.

CHAPTERS SIX AND SEVEN

6. Popkin, Michael H., Ph.D. *Active Parenting: Teaching Cooperation, Courage and Responsibility.* San Francisco: Harper San Francisco, 1987.

CHAPTER EIGHT

7. Popkin, Michael H., Ph.D. *Family Talk: A Video-Based Family Communication Program.* Atlanta: Active Parenting, Inc., 1989.

CHAPTER TEN

8. Caplan, Frank and Caplan, Theresa. *The Second Twelve Months of Life.* New York: The Putnam Publishing Group, 1982.

SUGGESTED READING

Albert, Linda and Popkin, Michael. *Quality Parenting*. New York: Random House, 1987.

Bradshaw, John. *Homecoming: Reclaiming and Championing Your Inner Child*. New York: Bantam Books, 1990.

Covey, Stephen R. *The 7 Habits of Highly Effective People: Powerful Lessons in Personal Change*. New York: A Fireside Book published by Simon & Schuster, 1989.

Curran, Dolores. *Stress and the Healthy Family*. New York: HarperCollins, 1987.

Curran, Dolores. *Traits of a Healthy Family*. San Francisco: Harper San Francisco, 1983.

Elkind, David. *The Hurried Child: Growing Up Too Fast Too Soon* (Revised Edition). New York: Addison-Wesley, 1988.

Miller, Alice. *For Your Own Good: Hidden cruelty in child-rearing and the roots of violence*. New York: Farrar, Straus, Giroux, 1984.

Popkin, Michael. *Active Parenting: Teaching Cooperation, Courage, and Responsibility*. San Francisco: Harper San Francisco, 1987.

Seuling, Barbara. *Who's the Boss Here? A Book About Parental Authority*. Racine, WI: A Golden Book published by Western Publishing Company, 1986.

INDEX

Enforcing
bedtime routine, 106
choices, 54, 77, 83, 128, 129, 133
consequences, 49, 96
discipline, 119
limits, 27, 105, 129
Environment, structuring your
child's, 85
Escalated tantrum, 118-119, 126,
128-132
Expectations, positive and negative,
27, 29-31, 34, 67, 111
Explanation, 126-127, 129, 131.
See also Action plan for Escalated
tantrum.
Eye contact, 11, 15, 42

Fantasy, 96-97
Fearfulness. *See* Bedtime.
Feelings. *See also* Emotions.
accepting your child's, 12-15, 20-
25, 99, 102
analyzing thoughts and, 57-67
in "I" message, 43
parent's, 58, 114, 118
in handling tantrums, 120-121,
123-125
in THINK, FEEL, DO cycle, 62-68
understanding, 10-14
validating, 13, 125
Fighting, 79, 128
Firmness, 81, 87, 105, 108-109, 133
Freedom within limits, 74
Frustrated tantrum, 117-118, 122-
123, 125, 131
Frustration(s), 15, 53, 70, 76, 93,
106, 127, 131. *See also* Emotions.

Goals, 15, 40, 56, 68, 113, 118, 136,
138
Growth
as a parent, 135
child's, 31, 73, 80, 96, 136
of relationship with child, 15, 59,
66

Guidance
in interaction with child, 135
of child, 81, 126
Guidelines to effective discipline, 40-
41

Helping your child, 14, 18, 24, 31,
36, 38, 44, 52, 56, 80, 97-100, 103,
105, 123
Helplessness, parent's feeling of, 124
Humiliation, 37
Humor, 121
Hysterics, 58-59, 66, 84

"I" Message, 28, 42-46, 48, 50, 93-94,
108, 110-114, 127-129
amended, 127-129
Imagination, 96, 105
Independence, 102, 118, 138
Infant(s) (Infancy), 11-13, 15, 25, 27,
29, 104-105, 118
Insecurity, 87. *See also* Security.
Instinctual reactions, 135-137
Interaction with your child, 21, 52,
72, 103-104, 135
Interdependence, 138
Isolation, 40. *See also* Punishment.

Kicking, 39, 41, 117, 119

Language, learning, 33
Lessons, 35-38, 55-56, 61-62, 67-69,
71-72, 77, 84-85, 113
Limits,
setting, 27-28, 46, 73-74, 77, 100,
105
testing, 111
Listening, 9-20, 23, 27, 29-30, 76-77,
93
Lying down with your child, 90.
See also Bedtime.

Manipulation, bedtime, 99,106
Manipulative tantrum, 119, 122,
129-131

WANTED: PEOPLE TO LEAD AN EXCITING

What is *Active Parenting Today: For 2 to 12 Year Olds*?

Active Parenting Today is a six-session video-based discussion program that uses a combination of learning methods that effectively strengthen and enrich the skills presented in this book. Because long-term understanding and success depend on involvement, *Active Parenting Today* is built around an interactive video/discussion format. The video vignettes humanize the content and spark interest with stories of realistic parent-child situations designed to draw you into the program and into the group discussion. Such involvement not only helps parents realize that they are not the only ones confronted by certain issues, but it also reinforces important parenting skills. The program includes 50 video scenes portrayed by families from a variety of ethnic and socioeconomic backgrounds.

Who Can Lead an *Active Parenting Today* Group?

Most Active Parenting leaders are helping professionals such as counselors, teachers, social workers, psychologists, ministers, nurses, and others. Some are concerned parents who enjoy leading group discussions and facilitating the activities that make Active Parenting the most advanced parent education program available anywhere. Some leaders prepare for leading their groups by participating in one of our optional one-day Active Parenting Publishers Leader Certification Workshops. Others prefer to rely on the detailed *Leader's Guide* and their own experience.

What Does The Program Offer That A Book Doesn't?

Visual reinforcement. Video shows as well as tells, and behavioral modeling is a powerful learning method. Video can help you better retain the skills that you have learned in this book. Our language is filled with phrases (like "seeing is believing") that highlight one fact: the majority of us are visual learners. In one study on learning attributed to Xerox, people retained only 10 percent of what they read, but 50 percent of what they saw. You will find that an Active Parenting group will help you remember what to do at that moment when you need it the most — namely, when *your* child is testing his or her limits.

NEW VIDEO-BASED PARENTING PROGRAM

Parents supporting parents. More and more parents are recognizing their need for skills, support, and information. When ten to twenty such parents gather together in an *Active Parenting Today* group with a concerned leader, something extraordinary happens. A sense of cohesiveness and mutual support develops. Parents come to understand that they are not alone with their doubts and difficulties in being parents. And best of all, they help each other learn, so that problems get solved and families grow stronger.

How Can You Get a Group Going in Your Community?

Most *Active Parenting Today* groups are sponsored by either a school, church or synagogue, mental health center, or private professional. If you want to make *Active Parenting Today* happen in your community, the first step is to contact someone in one of these organizations. That contact person should write us for an information packet that explains the program in detail. Then offer your support in helping to get the first *Active Parenting Today* group off the ground.

For Further Information Contact:

810 Franklin Court, Suite B
Marietta, GA 30067
1-800-825-0060

Over one million parents throughout the world have used Active Parenting Publishers parenting programs. We hope that your community will join us.

PARENTING HORIZONS

Julie A. Ross, M.A. runs Active Parenting workshops, support groups, and discussion groups in New York City. Parenting Horizons also offers several workshops and seminars. Currently available workshops include:

Active Parenting™

Video-based skills enhancement program teaches:
- Limit setting
- Instilling courage
- Understanding your child
- Developing responsibility
- Winning cooperation
- Family communication skills
- Enhancing self-esteem

Parents With Careers™

Video-based program for dual-career and single-parent families.

Family Talk™

Video-based seminars available on the following topics:
- Decision making in the family
- Television
- Okay to feel sad
- Money
- Stress
- What's a step-parent
- Honesty
- Teasing
- Grandparents
- Mother's time
- Feeling alone
- Mom's and Dad's time together
- Minorities
- Equality
- Choices

WORKSHOPS AND SEMINARS

Tantrums

This popular workshop covers the tantrum techniques developed by Ms. Ross and presented in this book.

Bedtime Blues

A workshop designed to help the parents of toddlers enforce bedtime and deal with specific bedtime issues.

Whining

Breaking a child from the habit of whining can be a frustrating task. This workshop discusses effective methods by which parents can teach their child proper communication techniques while diminishing the frequency of whining episodes.

Workshops are also available for professionals (teachers, daycare providers, camp counselors, etc.).

We believe that parent education is essential in today's society. As part of this commitment, we are happy to adapt our workshops and seminars to fit your needs and time constraints.

Ms. Ross is also available for private counseling, both in her office and by telephone nationwide.

For information about private counseling, joining a workshop, support group or discussion group, or booking a lecture, contact:

(212) 765-2377
www.parentinghorizons.com

or write to:

Julie A. Ross
c/o Excalibur Publishing
511 Avenue of the Americas
PMB 392
New York, NY 10011

152

About the Author

Julie A. Ross, M.A. has taught parenting courses and workshops for corporations, private organizations, the New York City public school system, private schools, and the YMCA. She currently teaches Active Parenting workshops and runs support groups in conjunction with Child's Play, a play-learning program at Central Presbyterian Church in New York City, and serves as Director of Education for Youth at St. Bartholomew's Church. Under the auspices of her company, Parenting Horizons, she conducts parent education workshops, counsels individuals and families, and is a certified Active Parenting group leader. She is a member of the American Counseling Association.